SUSTAINABLE FINANCING MECHANISMS FOR CORAL REEF CONSERVATION

Proceedings of a Workshop

Held at The World Bank
Washington, D.C.
June 23, 1995

Anthony J. Hooten and Marea E. Hatziolos, *Editors*

ESD

Environmentally Sustainable Development Proceedings Series No. 9
The World Bank, Washington, D.C.

First printing September 1995

This report has been prepared by the staff of the World Bank. The judgments expressed do
not necessarily reflect the views of the Board of Executive Directors or the governments
they represent.

Cover photograph by Jan Post. A queen angel fish in the Caribbean.

Anthony J. Hooten is a consultant to the World Bank. Marea E. Hatziolos is a coastal management
specialist in the Environment Department of the Bank.

ISBN 0-8213-3490-5

Contents

Preface

Coral reefs–the two words can generate a host of images and feelings: blue waters, colorful fish, strange-looking creatures, majestic coral colonies, bounties of food, treasure, and adventure.

Coral reefs are among the world's most biologically rich and productive ecosystems–the largest living structures on earth. These and related ecosystems such as mangroves, seagrass beds, and estuaries are a foundation of sustenance for much of the world's human population. Yet many coral reefs and adjoining coastal resources are in jeopardy of degradation and overexploitation.

Just as land and resource development must be environmentally sustainable to meet long-term objectives for improving human welfare, so conservation efforts must be financially sustainable to ensure long-term environmental protection and continuous benefits. Concern about the sustainable financing of marine conservation has grown with the realization that identifying solutions to problems is not enough. Actions must be initiated and sustained through continuous investments until conservation objectives are met. Traditional financing, such as public sector support, is generally not a viable option for long-term conservation. Governments alone are unable to provide full support for conservation and sustainable use. While start-up funds for establishment of conservation efforts are often forthcoming, economic uncertainty and competing demands on public budgets limit the level of investment for operations and maintenance. Shifting political support for the environmental agenda, in both industrial and developing countries, can prevent the long-range planning required for sustainable management of coral reefs and associated marine systems.

Financing conservation efforts requires mixed strategies that involve combinations of approaches and partnerships. For developing countries, this may include a mix of grants and loans, new approaches to revenue generation (including user fees), the development of public-private partnerships, and community-based co-management arrangements that build on local incentives.

Sustainable financing of coral reef conservation applies not only to marine protected areas, as described in the four-volume study jointly produced by the Great Barrier Reef Marine Park Authority, the World Bank, and the World Conservation Union (IUCN), *A Global Representative System of Marine Protected Areas*. It must encompass efforts outside protected areas, where the bulk of development activities affecting the productivity and health of coral reefs take place.

The proceedings that follow–from a one-day workshop held at the World Bank on June 23, 1995–explore these issues in the context of strategies for sustainable financing of coral reef conservation, although they apply to other important coastal and marine ecosystems as well. The purpose of the proceedings is to continue dialogue with private sector interests, investment agencies, and nongovernmental organizations (NGOs), as well as with governments and the International Coral Reef Initiative, to identify the conditions necessary for sustainable financing of marine conservation. Contact information for each of the panelists and workshop participants is also included. Readers are encouraged to contact individuals with questions and comments and to develop an active network. Only through continued discussion, networking, and support can these ideas be turned into practical applications and help sustain these critical ecosystems.

Anthony J. Hooten and Marea E. Hatziolos

Acknowledgments

The workshop on Sustainable Financing Mechanisms for Coral Reef Conservation and its *Proceedings* are the result of many people's efforts. The workshop organizers were encouraged early on by the very positive reponse to the sustainable financing theme from colleagues and practitioners in the field. Resources and staff support from the Vice Presidency for Environmentally Sustainable Development and its Land, Water, and Natural Habitats Division helped translate the idea into a well-organized and highly successful event. Much of the workshop's success was due to the diverse perspectives and experience of its participants, who provided timely presentations and lively discussion throughout. Last but not least, sincere thanks are due to Ismail Serageldin for his initial and continuing support to the workshop and its objectives and his active participation in the event and its follow-up.

The editors wish to thank the panelists for their written submissions, which have been edited for publication. Special thanks go to Jan Post for providing his underwater photographs and to Joyce Petruzzelli for the cover design. The editors are also grateful to Katherin Golitzen and Michael Watkins for desktopping of the manuscript. Alicia Hetzner, Virginia Hitchcock, Helen Meade, and Ivan Radan aided in the production process.

Keynote Address

Ismail Serageldin
Environmentally Sustainable Development
World Bank

Ladies and gentlemen and fellow coral reef lovers, it is a privilege to welcome you to the World Bank and a pleasure to be with you here today. This gathering has two basic objectives:

1. To share our experiences about the management of coral reefs and especially the sustainable financing of coral reef conservation

2. To take concrete steps towards implementation of more effective conservation efforts.

Concrete action, however, will require a clearly defined course of action, and raising the consciousness of many about the importance of coral reefs in terms of global biodiversity conservation.

All who are present here today know how important coral reefs are. But that is not enough! We must convince many others of the importance of our concerns. We must get others to share these concerns. We must be able communicate to others, nonspecialists and decisionmakers, the urgency of the needed actions. For while all of us may be convinced of these questions, there is a tide of complacency and disengagement out there unlike anything we have witnessed in the last twenty years.

The Problem

Coral reefs, among the most biologically diverse and most productive ecosystems on earth, are in serious decline globally. Despite the efforts of legendary figures like Captain Cousteau, to whom we wish a happy 85th birthday and who is represented here today by the Vice President of the Cousteau Society, Paula DiPerna; of Graeme Kelleher and his colleagues at the Great Barrier Reef Marine Park Authority; and of IUCN and many other institutions, governments and individuals, the public remains sadly unaware of the importance of coral reefs or their plight.

Compared to the global efforts underway to stem the tide of tropical deforestation and the loss of terrestrial biodiversity, little attention has been, or is being, paid to the unfolding tragedy taking place beneath the surface and along the coasts of the world's tropical seas.

This is doubly troubling. Recently, the scientific community has drawn attention to the fact that at the higher taxonomic level, there is much more biodiversity in the sea than on land. In other words, if an objective choice had to be made between preserving the terrestrial and the marine biodiversity on the basis of the desire to keep the largest variety of basically different life forms, the choice would definitively favor the marine realm. That, my friends, is not a generally known fact, much less an accepted fact, outside of a small community of specialists.

Again, my friends, we must reach out to others. It is not enough to talk among ourselves. I know that thanks to the efforts of many of the people and institutions represented in this room, much more attention is being paid to the plight of coral reefs and the need to conserve these systems for future generations. The recent US-supported International Coral Reef Initiative is a major step forward, much more still needs to be done.

Beyond the public awareness and attention, however, action is required. Action must be based on a sound diagnosis of the causes of the problems and on a clear course of action to be pursued: targeted, effective and sustainable. Let's take each of these in turn.

Diagnosis: Identifying the Causes of the Problem

The causes of the stresses on the marine coral reef systems are varied: although natural events, such as storms, predator infestation and disease, can have a significant impact on coral reef ecosystems, these periodic disturbances are part of the normal stresses and strains of coral reef communities, which have evolved mechanisms to cope with such stress. It is *human activity* that is the primary agent of degradation of these ecosystems.

The main threats to coral reefs can roughly be divided into three categories: physical destruction, pollution, and over-exploitation. Habitat destruction is the main threat to terrestrial biodiversity whereas over-exploitation and pollution are probably more important in coral reefs.

Among the most important impacts are:

- Direct impacts from activities such as resource extraction, dredging and filling, over-harvesting, recreation, and pollution from land-based activities including point and non-point sources such as municipal waste, industrial effluent and agricultural runoff

- Inadequate planning and management of coastal areas and their watersheds

- Looming in the background, the potential adverse effects of global climate change, including global warming, which may, through higher seawater temperature and increased precipitation and storm activities, place additional stress on threatened systems.

These stresses are likely to continue. Population growth rates in the coastal zone (5 to 6 percent in many tropical countries) along with increasing use of coral reef resources, is intensifying pressure on coral reefs and accelerating their rate of decline worldwide. These populations are frequently very poor and their livelihoods must be secured in non-destructive ways if the conservation efforts are to be successful.

Such chronic forms of human-induced stress can lower the resilience of coral reef ecosystems to natural disturbances, setting in motion processes that may be difficult if not impossible to reverse.

The skeptical will ask me "How much?" "Have you measured it?" No, I do not know exactly, nor can I say for sure, but there is no evidence, anecdotal or otherwise, that would lead one to be complacent. Reefbase, an important effort at global monitoring of coral reefs–itself under stress from budget cutters in donor agencies–will help, over time, to get a handle on such issues. Surely, however, the course of practical wisdom is to slow down the destruction and protect the most valuable resources *now*.

For example: The stress from human activities (over-fishing of herbivores and eutrophication from coastal pollution–favoring the proliferation of algae on reefs) in combination with periodic natural disturbance (such as hurricanes–which can clear vast areas of live coral cover–and epidemics, which may wipe out key species like algal-grazing sea urchins) is thought to be responsible for the demise of Jamaica's coral reefs–once among the most lush in the Caribbean.

What Is Being Done

Targeting priority interventions

After the establishment of the Global Environment Facility (GEF), the Bank became increasingly involved in biodiversity conservation. The Scientific and Technical Advisory Panel of the GEF has determined that 15 to 20 percent of all biodiversity funding should go to coastal and marine biodiversity conservation. Thus far, investment in marine biodiversity has lagged far behind terrestrial biodiversity projects. This is not surprising, because in the terrestrial realm there were numerous projects "ready to go," and there was considerable consensus on where the most important areas lie. In the sea we were largely empty handed.

Now we have a report guiding investment in marine biodiversity conservation and, not surprisingly, a major part of this report concerns itself with coral reefs. The report allows us to target interventions and identify some priorities worldwide. The next presentation will explain its purpose and contents. This report has been a major achievement, the first of its kind ever prepared, and I heartily congratulate IUCN, the Great Barrier Reef Marine Park Authority (GBRMPA), and my colleagues at the World Bank. I would like to extend personal thanks to everyone who has contributed to its production, in particular Graeme Kelleher and Chris Bleakley. There is also the beautiful poster map which draws the attention to the importance of marine biodiversity conservation and to the existence and contents of the report.

But the proof of the pudding is not in its recipe but in its eating. In other words, can we make marine reserves work?

Effectiveness

We will not be able to protect the parks by police measures alone. They cannot be kept just as playgrounds for the rich in the face of mounting poverty among the growing populations in the coastal zone.

Effectiveness will require building a broad constituency recognizing the interest of each stakeholder (as was done by the GBRMPA). Effectiveness will require that we deal with the poor, the marginalized and indigenous people and give them a vested economic interest in protecting the parks from pollution and exploitation (as was done in Ras Mohammed).

Effectiveness, therefore, also involves outreach–the role of NGOs, building of partnerships, building of coalitions on the ground and in the halls of power. It is all about reaching out to others, not just going with our technical knowledge.

The Challenge of Sustainable Financing

The World Bank report *People and Parks* identifies inadequate and unsustainable funding as one of the main reasons for the failure of reserves. There are excellent examples of coral reef protection which have worked very well, largely because a sustainable source of financing has been created. The marine reserve pays for itself. I have seen how well this works in Bonaire in the Netherlands Antilles and have dived on the Great Barrier Reef, arguably the best managed Large Marine Ecosystem in the world. In my own country, Egypt, there are major efforts to preserve the fantastic biodiversity resources of the Sinai and Red Sea coasts. Mike Pearson, who is here, just informed me that the fee structure and fund arrangements have been implemented in Egypt, making Ras Mohammed a self-financing (sustainable) affair.

There are reasons for optimism, probably more so than for many terrestrial ecosystems. One of the reasons, the one we are going to discuss today, is that there really is great scope for revenue generation based on non-extractive use.

Most of the conservation literature is about what should and could be done. There is little on the financing of the recommended activities and even less on the important qualifier: sustainable financing. Too many conservation projects collapse eventually, because they have a finite timespan for financing.

We need to mobilize and sustain investments in conservation and wise use from a variety of sources. We need first: the commitment of the host government. Second: we need to build partnerships with the private sector, with communities, nongovernmental organizations and individuals. These partnerships should initiate and sustain activities that not only generate revenues for conservation and management of coral reefs, but also alleviate the source of much of the human-induced pressure on reefs. This can be done through family planning programs, provision of alternative livelihoods, low-impact but profitable use strategies (for example, eco-tourism, mariculture, marine bioprospecting), integrated coastal zone management and economic instruments. All of these will be subjects in today's discussions.

We hope that today will be the beginning of a continuing dialogue among coral reef managers, conservationists, scientists, economists, members of the private sector, the international development community and micro-enterprise developers, on ways to make coral reef conservation a self-sustaining and profitable endeavor. We in the Bank will be anxious to hear your ideas and to lend our support to refining and implementing those ideas which hold out the most promise in meeting this challenge.

The Role of the World Bank

You may well ask what is the World Bank doing? What can it do? There are several ways in which the World Bank can assist in the protection of coral reefs.

- The needs of some coral reef reserves could be financed through normal Bank loans or IDA credits. To the extent that host governments are willing to borrow, we could also prefinance the preparation of such projects through the Project Preparation Facility.

- GEF grants are also a possibility about which we will hear more.

- Through its policy dialogue with Governments, the Bank can advocate measures for the protection of marine biodiversity. We have, after all, tackled through dialogue difficult issues such as downsizing the civil service, changing the trade regime and enhancing opportunities for the private sector. We should be able to engage in dialogue on behalf of coral reefs.

- Indirectly, Bank loans may benefit coral reefs through financing of pollution abatement projects, watershed management and alternative livelihoods for people trapped in the vicious circle of poverty and environmental degradation.

- More recently, Integrated Coastal Zone Management was identified as a major tool for coral reef protection by the Coral Reef Conference sponsored by the International Coral Reef Initiative (ICRI) and held in the Philippines a few weeks ago. Coastal zone management has also become a part of the Bank's activities, and the Environment Department's Division of Land, Water and Natural Habitats is the focal point for our efforts in this area.

Desirable Outcomes of the Workshop

So, before the end of the day, we hope to have:

- Enriched each other by identification of recent, successful experience in raising money from users and other interested groups to support conservation of marine ecosystems

- Moved from the individual lessons learned to a wider application of these experiences in the field, to evaluate what works and what doesn't. We need a commitment from everyone here to support the piloting and testing of good ideas that will emerge in your deliberations

- Generated a consensus on sustainable financing approaches that map out an active partnership between government, local communities and private interests (that is, the Ras Mohammed model).

Although focused on marine environments, the lessons learned from today's discussion on partnerships, mobilizing resources and building political will, can send a powerful positive message about effective financing of ESD, the theme of our Third Annual World Bank Conference scheduled for October 4-6, 1995, and I will personally bring these findings to the attention of the Finance Ministers and their staffs.

Conclusions

By an unfortunate irony, while confidence in the importance of environmental aspects as an integral part of development has been strongly affirmed, the development enterprise–itself a vital and indispensable endeavor in global terms–is under attack. The very idea of a beneficial role for governments, and the idea of development cooperation between North and South are being assailed. So, while we can all be justifiably proud of what we have achieved in conceptual and operational terms, we must redouble our efforts in the face of diminished development assistance budgets, on behalf of all the dedicated and successful efforts of so many present here and elsewhere, who have been combining conservation and development. We must not allow the failure of politicized aid that was labeled as development assistance, or the occasional failed project of the past, to overshadow the success stories achieved by so many. We must join forces with friends and allies to roll back the tide of doubt that threatens the world's development enterprise. If we fail, the worst-hit victims will not be development institutions or research centers and the dedicated men and women within them. The real victims will be the natural ecosystems and the weakest in human society–the poor, the hungry, the unemployed and the marginalized. Even more, the future generations will not only be deprived of the marvels of the coral reefs and the marine ecosystems that support them, but will inherit polluted waters, unhealthy air, parched fields and eroded soils. We must not fail.

Consider, as you deliberate over the ideas and proposals that will be presented by the various panelists, the paradox of our times. We live in a world of plenty, of dazzling scientific advances and technological breakthroughs. Adventures in cyberspace are at hand. The Cold War is over, and with that we were offered the hope of global stability.   Yet, our times are marred by conflict, violence, debilitating economic uncertainties and tragic poverty. And now so many of the rich want to turn their backs on the poor. Selfish concerns seem to displace enlightened self interest, for we are all downwind or downstream of each other. This is more than ever a time for an united front of the caring.

Poverty and environmental degradation go hand in hand, for it is the poor who frequently are the unwitting vectors of environmental degradation as well as the victims of its consequences.

Today, in the 47 "least developed" countries of the world, 10 percent of the world's population subsists on less than 0.5 percent of the world's income. Some 40,000 people die from hunger related causes every day. Many of the poor who survive lack access to the fundamental needs of a decent existence. Over a billion people are compelled to live on less than a dollar a day. A sixth or more of the human family lives a marginalized existence. Seventy percent of the world population lives within 100 kilometers of the sea. Attacking the poverty and unsound economic activities in the coastal zones is an integral part of protecting the coral reefs.

Therein lies the challenge before us. Will we accept such human degradation as inevitable? Or will we strive to help–in Franz Fanon's evocative phrase–"the wretched of the earth?" Will we accept that we are no longer responsible for future generations, or will we try to act as true stewards of the earth? I have no doubt of what your response will be. But the response must be in bringing your knowledge to bear in identifying the road map for practical action and to convince others for the need for such action. So, together, let us think of the unborn, remember the forgotten, give hope to the forlorn, and reach out to the unreached, and by wise actions today lay the foundation for better tomorrows.

     SUSTAINABLE FINANCING MECHANISMS FOR CORAL REEF CONSERVATION

I. A Global Representative System of Marine Protected Areas

Introduction

Jan Post, Environment Department
World Bank

Shortly after the World Bank's Environment Department was established, biodiversity became an area of great interest. A symposium on the subject of biodiversity was organized; however, surprisingly little attention was initially given to the area of marine biodiversity. In the early stages, the Bank's role in biodiversity conservation was difficult to define. The challenge was to join finance with scientific rigor and action, with results realized in a reasonable timespan. In the late 1980s and early 1990s, a series of workshops was held and proposals solicited. The Bank decided to build on existing activity and adopt an ongoing IUCN program. Using 18 groups world-wide, IUCN was identifying priority areas for marine conservation. The effort has resulted in the production of the report we are launching today: *A Global Representative System of Marine Protected Areas.* How the report can contribute to future conservation efforts is discussed by the representatives on this panel.

History of the Marine Protected Areas Report

Graeme Kelleher
The World Conservation Union Marine Programs

A Global Representative System of Marine Protected Areas (MPAs). What does the term mean? It means a representative of every kind of marine ecosystem that exists in the sea. These four volumes represent a combination of nine years work by three institutions–the World Conservation Union (IUCN), the Great Barrier Reef Marine Park Authority (GBRMPA) and The World Bank. The program started in 1975 when IUCN recognized the problem of potential threat to the integrity of much of the world's marine resources. In 1979 the GBRMPA realized it as well. In the First General Assembly of IUCN, a resolution was adopted to work toward creation of a global representative system of MPAs. In that same year a resolution was passed by the World Wilderness Congress in Colorado.

The next step involved development of guidelines that have been shown to work in practice in creating MPAs in previous areas. The guidelines were published by IUCN in 1990. Following this, 18 working groups were established, which together covered all the world's coastal areas. Recognizing the important dichotomy between the two disciplines, the working groups were deliberately comprised of scientists and managers working together. During meetings among several of the 18 working groups, especially in developing countries, we realized that the dichotomy occurs equally in the developing world; in many cases it was the first time that the two groups had ever communicated with one another. This process has reinforced the notion that communities working together, both bottom-up and top-down, is the only way that progress will be achieved–not one or the other.

The charges to each of the working groups were:

- *Divide their particular regions into their biogeographical zones.* We asked that each of the groups use the biogeographic classification historically used in their region. The region was based on previous data collected using the original classifications. Any new ideal scheme would mean that data would have to be translated and therefore, not be immediately useful for analysis.

- *Identify the six highest priorities either for creation of new MPAs or establishment of management in existing, paper parks.* One of the major criteria used in the development of the priorities was feasibility, or practicality. We were determined that the recommendations would be achievable in practice, and not a collection of wish lists based only on purely scientific or ecological criteria. However, these were also given weight in the process of identifying priorities.

It is important to recognize what this report is and is not. Essentially it is pragmatic–representing the best judgment of working groups of scientists and managers–regarding the highest priorities for the establishment of new marine protected areas, or the development of effective management in those many marine protected areas that are not managed properly. However, MPAs are not ends unto themselves. They are only one important tool in the suite of measures necessary to maintain biological diversity and to sustain fisheries in national and international waters.

Perhaps the greatest threat to the sea comes from the land in the form of land-based sources of pollution. The critical deficiency in marine management is the absence of integrated decisionmaking in both the land and the sea. Integrated coastal zone management is now widely recognized, and explicitly so by IUCN, as an approach that offers the best hope of conserving the world's marine resources in the face of incentives to over-exploit them, resulting in what has been called "the tragedy of the commons."

Conservation efforts through integrated coastal zone management will have to provide for some areas to be protected as reservoirs of biodiversity, high productivity, or areas critical in the life cycle of marine organisms, including fished species. Large marine protected areas, such as the GBRMP, actually constitutes integrated coastal zone management, and are vital to marine resource sustainability.

Reports only have value if their recommendations are translated into real action– on the ground and in the sea. It will be a challenge to financing institutions and governments to determine whether the immense work embodied in this report is wasted or utilized for the benefit of the natural environment and for human communities. How will the recommendation in this report be implemented? We need clear courses of actions.

We now must develop a coherent plan which will be applied to all of the 18 major regions of the world's seas. These 18 working groups constitute a vital resource which will be used to develop country-specific or regional proposals for MPAs, based on the report's recommendations. The quality of the product will depend on whether enough resources are available to bring people with the skills and experience necessary into the planning process. Without proper planning, projects fail.

The challenge facing financing institutions and governments will be to provide the investment funds which will allow these proposals, not only to sustain the marine environment, but to sustain the human communities that depend on the sea. Sustainable financing is a necessary ingredient in achieving ecologically sustainable use of the world's seas. Marine protected areas can contribute to such financing, both by revenue generated by tourism, and by increasing the sustainable harvest from fished areas, either adjacent to small MPAs or within large, multiple use MPAs (for example, the Florida Keys).

Now is the time for financial institutions, governments, and communities to implement these recommendations for the sake of the world's seas, and the people who depend upon their resources.

Mentoring for Sustainability

Richard Kenchington, External Services
Great Barrier Reef Marine Park Authority

With the advent of this workshop and the presentation of this report, we have the illusion of moving rapidly. We have passed two major milestones for the conservation and sustainable use of coral reefs. That is, the MPA report and International Coral Reef Initiative (ICRI) kick-off meeting in Dumagette City, Philippines, resulting in the development of the *Framework For Action* for the conservation of the world's coral reefs. These two milestones are closely linked and complementary processes. Whether we can pass the next two milestones as quickly is fairly doubtful.

To achieve the future desired outcomes we must plan, building from the recommendations of the MPA report and framework from the ICRI. These do not set specific action plans as such, but rather, sets of criteria that leave room for regions to develop frameworks that suit their needs and styles of operation, so they can develop solutions that they own and are committed to implementing. The ultimate goal is to develop national plans that can be successfully implemented on the ground.

My experience is that one of the most complex parts of this process is developing bankable proposals. Many, particularly the smaller governments, perceive project funding as a hurdle or examination, and that only through proper scoring can they hope to benefit.

Five years is a considered a long time for economists; yet five years is a very short time for ecologists, who prefer to work in time spans closer to fifty years. Based on experience in Australia, in a very favorable environment, it takes ten years to get a Marine Protected Area system up and running to the extent that it begins to appear viable for sustainability. However, if you take off the pressure and lose momentum–it creates a flash in the pan situation (that is, paper parks) that may be worse than never having started at all. Therefore, it is critical that MPA designation become established through processes such as "mentoring." Mentoring can be analogous to supporting students in the preparation of their theses and papers: strong background support, while the student develops solutions, thereby preserving a sense of ownership in the process. In the cases of Marine Protected Areas there is a need to advocate mentoring through: (1) regional workshops, and (2) frameworks.

Coral reefs are a great symbol of the problem of the coastal zone–they are the canary in the cage. Given the importance of the many associated and supporting ecosystems in the marine environment, we must remember that we are using coral reefs as a symbol of the whole. However, we need to use coral reefs to develop Integrated Coastal Zone Management solutions–for a very simple reason: a large proportion of the human population in coastal developing countries, particularly in the tropics, depend upon coastal marine resources for the majority of their digestible protein. Every time we take a short-term, social, economic or political fix, which destroys or reduces those resources at a time when population is increasing, we get an increasingly intractable social, political and economic solution.

Conservation–the protection and sustainable use of reefs and coastal zones, is not a luxury or aesthetic option–a way in which it has been treated in many economic forums. It is a fundamental part of the future economic life of coastal countries. We have a massive education program ahead of us. To get there, we need to have regional workshops, in which we facilitate mentoring in developing regional strategies. We then need to go with nations that are focused and enthusiastic to national approaches which develop national commitment right across the sectors–fishing, policing, financing to get a project which is indeed finance-able. We need projects in the field which relate to the national framework and are supported by it, and not just seen as a side show.

To use an example from Australia, it's a matter of turning "heyottas" into "gunnadoos." We tended to have in the early days of the [Great Barrier] reef people who would say "heyotta do this" and "heyotta do that" and "heyotta do something else." It was always "they ought to" not "we ought to." The message is: we have to get from "they ought to do this" to "we are going to do that"–a "gunnadoo"–"we're gunnadoo it." With the right financing, the right support through mentoring, which puts the local people in charge through ownership and responsibility, some of the recommendations from this MPA report can be turned into sustainable action.

A Cooperative Program to Implement the Marine Protected Areas Report

Chris Bleakley, External Services
The Great Barrier Reef Marine Park Authority

The foundation for the report, *A Global Representative System of Marine Protected Areas*, is a marine management network through CNPPA–a regional network of working groups comprised of managers and scientists, representatives of government and nongovernment communities. We believe this composition makes the network ideally suited for developing biodiversity conservation through international waters project proposals, and in implementing the recommendations in the report. An important linkage has been established with the ICRI's *Framework for Action*. Some initial support is available to IUCN through the U.S. government to use the marine management network in contributing to the ICRI process, and participate in the ICRI regional workshops.

The aim of this network and partnering is to facilitate on-the-ground action. We hope to emerge from this process with country-driven proposals for the GEF and other donors that implement recommendations of the report and priorities identified for ICRI.

We are also building other important partnerships which will assist in implementing the report's recommendations. One of the key initiatives is the Regional Seas program of UNEP. In the eastern Asian Seas, we are working with UNEP's coordinating body, COBSEA, to develop a regional GEF proposal to implement report priorities and develop marine management capacity in many countries of that region. In the south Pacific, we are working closely with the South Pacific Regional Environmental Program to develop a similar initiative. We are also working with UNEP's Southeast Pacific Commission to cooperate in a regional workshop that will bring managers and scientists together to develop project proposals that also implement report recommendations.

Our approach is to catalyze and enable country-driven initiatives, through supplementing and strengthening local expertise. We aim to rely on the motivation of local communities and people rather than financial reward. Developing the in-country capacity for management is perhaps the single greatest step that can be taken to implement the recommendations in the report.

Marine Protected Areas in Belize

Sue Wells
United Nations Development Programme

Belize is a very nice example of how some of the issues discussed at this workshop can be put into practice. Belize has long been considered an experimental site for conservation organizations, scientists and managers to try their ideas in the field.

In some ways Belize is a special case, given the level of attention it has received. Coral reefs of Belize are the mainstay for the government, through tourism and fisheries. The first marine protected area (MPA) was Half Moon Caye, established in the late 1960s or early 1970s. However, there has been no active management of Half Moon Caye. Although it has been declared as a protected area, money is still not available to develop a management plan. Even in the face of donor activity in Belize, we are still relying upon voluntary support for developing management plans and other on-the-ground activities vital to management of the reef.

In Belize a variety of legislation can be used to protect coral reefs. The Ministry of Natural Resources covers parks and protected areas, and fisheries legislation allows for the formation of marine reserves. Half Moon Caye was established under the Ministry of Natural Resources, and Hol Chan Marine Reserve was established under the Fisheries Department. These two government agencies have different approaches to protecting marine resources. The Ministry of Natural Resources identifies an area that is considered appropriate for conservation, and once boundaries have been established, it can be designated with little or no ground work. However, requirement for a management plan follows designation. As a result, there are a number of paper parks in Belize.

Under the Fisheries legislation, boundaries can also be established for park/protected area designation; however, the policy of the Fisheries Department has been that designation should not be declared until a management plan has been prepared, along with funding and resources for management. Therefore, Hol Chan Marine Reserve was designated after a management plan and funding were established. Only then did the government appoint fisheries officers to enforce the Reserve. Recent feedback from some of the donor agencies considering new protected areas in Belize is that *a priori* park designation is preferred before additional funds are granted to support management plans. Consequently, the Fisheries Department is currently weighing the pros and cons of designating an area before management plans and financing strategies are in place.

The establishment of parks and protected areas in Belize is seen as an integral part of Coastal Zone Management plan development. As part of the Fisheries Department, the Coastal Zone Management Unit has developed most of the marine protected area initiatives in Belize. In 1993, the UNDP/GEF program was initiated, and the Marine Protected Areas Program has been an integral part. Although not yet designated as a World Heritage Site, there is strong political will for this action.

The basis of a national system of protected areas is available in Belize. Twenty areas have been identified, eight of which include coral reefs; others include mangrove and in-shore lagoon habitats. However, there is a bottleneck. It has been relatively easy to get funding agencies, consultants and scientists to do the ground work for these protected areas (that is, existing conditions, draft management plans).   The main problem is how to move ahead with implementation and management. The hurdle is a lack of people in Belize, either within the government, or within national NGOs, to carry this effort forward. The Coastal Zone Management Unit presently has only one government employee. The other staff receive support from external funding. Three NGOs are active within the marine environment, and are looked to for assistance through efforts such as co-management of protected areas, assistance with monitoring and education.

It is hoped that at the local level, MPAs in Belize can be made financially viable. A proposal currently at the cabinet level is considering a conservation tax for tourists and visitors (about US$10) that could be paid into a protected areas trust fund.

The Hol Chan Marine Reserve is now being managed out of its own trust fund; however, this does not include the salaries for the staff. The current GEF project is examining the institutional arrangements for sustaining the Coastal Zone Management efforts and Marine Protected Areas, once established. However, the project only runs until 1998. Thus, these examples illustrate many of the issues to be addressed in this workshop.

Question: I fully support some planning–as someone said, it is probably 90 percent of getting the work done. But a lot is happening on the ground, and it was not clear whether you are planning from the ground up. Secondly, in Volume Two [of the report]–and forgive me if there is some cynicism–but on page 22 with the USAID training strategy, for example, the study results are in preparation of eight volumes of background material, and the proposal was never funded. Could you convince us that within these four volumes, something [has] happened on the ground?

Response: (Graeme Kelleher). To address the second question first, we are all in a position similar to the Caribbean. The actual funding of producing these reports amounted to 10 percent of the real cost. So 90 percent of the time spent in producing these reports was voluntary. The fundamental question is: "Can we convince financial institutions and governments to provide the resources to implement the recommendations on the ground?" I have no doubt at all that there will be some successes, and some failures. All that we can do is what we can do–our best. Most of us are operating voluntarily; some of us are being paid. But we can't do more than that. IUCN hasn't the resources to guarantee that a particular recommendation will be carried out in the field.

I understood the first question to be whether there will be recognition of the need for projects to be built from the bottom up. From the very start, that is why we had 18 regional working groups rather than someone in Gland, Switzerland [IUCN] or Washington, D.C. telling people what they should do. We got the communities to recommend what should be done. To the extent that IUCN remains involved in the rest of this program, this approach will be the foundation. For example, in the GBRMPA, we had an absolute rule: an officer going to another developing nation to assist in developing a proposal [for MPA designation] could never be the project officer. The project officer had to come from the country. And this approach is something we have always been committed to.

Response [to an unintelligible question concerning priority setting in the MPA report]: (Richard Kenchington). Because we went through the process of 18 regional working groups, the reports from the regions reflect views of where those regions were the time. The North Atlantic region, and the structure of its operation, was ready to identify priorities at national and regional levels compared to some of the other regions. There is also the factor that there were varying degrees of cynicism–the degree and the extent to which people felt it was worth getting involved varied considerably. I think that is reflected in the recommendations.   I have no doubt that these recommendations are an extremely good basis from which to start, but as the regional groups work further, we will see the [recommendations] evolve and reflect greater belief in the process. As we know within Indonesia, that belief is growing very rapidly. The underlying message is: if you see things in the report that are not there but should be, it is a case of working in the regions and through the regions (that is, bottom up) to make sure it [designation] happens.

Comment: (Chris Bleakley). It is also important to remember that each report has been developed by a regional working group, and are designed to stand alone regionally. Because there is no accepted global classification system, it has not been possible to compare between regions.

II. Financing and Sustaining Coral Reef Conservation Initiatives

Introduction

John Dixon, Environment Department
World Bank

Many of the papers, throughout the panel discussions, deal with the same sets of issues–questions of identifying benefits, finding funds, and securing financing for innovative ways that can be used increasingly to conserve protected areas, such as coral reefs. With respect to economic importance, if coral reefs are so valuable, so precious and unique, then why aren't dollars forthcoming to protect them? If such resources are so valuable, then markets should work. In fact, markets do not work in all cases. There are differences between the more narrowly defined financial benefits from using coral reef resources, in terms of direct use, versus a much wider range of social benefits.

The good news is that much is being done to both identify the types of benefits and costs that are involved, and to actually start capturing them. Much of what is presented below are such lessons from the field.

In pursuing this goal, several actions are needed. We need to recognize the types of benefits–the wide variety of benefits that come from the sustainable management of coral reefs. We need to do a better job of capturing those benefits –the money for sustainable finance. We also need to recognize the cost of inaction–the fact that without management, without taking steps, the cost to societies, economies, individuals, and to the global ecosystem can be very large.

The focus of this workshop is taking that important next step–from identifying important ecosystems and protected areas, to actually capturing benefits in terms of securing funding from different groups to support management. The issue is fundamentally a matter of mobilizing support. And the support comes from different groups–governments, local communities, and in many cases, users can be valuable sources of support. Some examples have already been given (that is, The Great Barrier Reef Marine Park); however, much of the work on securing local-level support has come from examples in the Caribbean. There are a number of panelists who have been involved with many of these case studies.

In conclusion, a very important dimension in mobilizing economics resources is recognizing the benefits, the cost of inaction, and forming the necessary partnerships between governments, users, NGOs, and others. Fortunately, all are represented in the summaries below.

Revenue Generation to Sustain Coral Reef Conservation

Tighe Geoghegan
Caribbean Natural Resources Institute

With well-managed and fully self-financing marine protected areas in three territories of the region (Saba Marine Park, Bonaire Marine Park, and the marine protected areas of the British Virgin Islands), the Caribbean may be leading the way in local financing of coral reef conservation. In all of these territories, the revenue generation strategies employed are based on user fees levied on scuba divers and, in the case of the British Virgin Islands, yacht charters as well. The success of these strategies has been largely dependent on a high level of collaboration between the protected area managers and the commercial users of the marine protected areas; that is, the dive operators and charter boat companies. In every case, the fees are actually collected by the commercial users, who also share other tasks related to administering the systems.

Elsewhere in the insular Caribbean, only the marine protected areas in the U.S. and French territories, which are highly subsidized by their national governments, can be described as adequately managed. As the negative effects of recreational use, over-fishing, and (perhaps most critically) improper controls over coastal and watershed development are becoming more obvious on the region's coral reefs, many other countries in the Caribbean are considering development of marine protected areas as a mechanism for reef conservation. In virtually every case, economic realities require that these protected areas be self-financing. In theory, this should pose little problem in any country in which coral reefs and other marine resources are an important recreational and tourism attraction. Visitor surveys which have been conducted in several countries of the Caribbean have all indicated a high willingness to pay for entry into well-managed marine protected areas and for the use of such management-related amenities as mooring buoys. The actual fee levels at the marine parks in Saba, Bonaire, and the British Virgin Islands remain considerably below the average which visitors would be willing to pay, yet are still enough to fully cover management costs.

Earlier this month, the Caribbean Natural Resources Institute hosted a regional workshop on revenue generation strategies for protected areas. Of the fourteen participants from nine Caribbean countries, twelve were involved in the development of coastal and marine protected areas. During the workshop, participants examined the requirements for making these marine protected areas financially self-sufficient, and sought solutions to a number of problems and constraints, which appear to be relevant to other tropical regions of the world.

The most critical obstacles are faced by government departments charged with the development and management of marine protected areas, because they generally lack the institutional ability to collect and manage revenues. When fee systems are implemented, the revenue generally must go into the government's consolidated fund (described by the workshop participants as "the black hole"). The management agency is then provided by government with a budget which may have no relation, except a negative one, with the amount of revenue being collected. Thus, the level of management is never able to match the level of use. Several workshop participants noted that even when governments had the flexibility to establish earmarked funds, they were often not permitted to do so as a requirement of the restructuring of their loan agreements with the international lending institutions. (Thus, those hosting this meeting today may actually be contributing to the problem that we have gathered to address.)

Because of these constraints, most countries are exploring the establishment of statutory bodies (such as national trusts or national parks authorities) which would have a level of independence from government and would be legally and administratively able to levy fees and manage revenues. In Jamaica, plans are underway to divest the management of the country's marine parks (presently there is only one, Montego Bay Marine Park, but others are now being planned) to local institutions with fiduciary powers.

In St. Lucia, a collaborative management arrangement has been established between the government and a community institution with the capability of managing the protected area and administering a fee system. Fees will be placed in a separate government fund from which payments will be made quarterly to the community institution for the management of the protected area. While the arrangement appears to have an excellent chance of success in this specific case, it may not be repeatable in other areas of the country which do not have well-established local institutions, thus constraining the growth of the planned national system of marine protected areas.

To guard against fluctuations in visitor levels, entry and user fees can and should be supplemented by other financing mechanisms, which can range from grants and government subsidies through membership clubs (for example, "The Friends of the Marine Park") and souvenir sales. It has generally been the case in the Caribbean that capital and start-up costs have been covered through bi- and multi-lateral grants and soft loans. Therefore, it has not been necessary to factor in these one-time costs when setting fee levels.

In summary, entry and recreational user fees are feasible and effective mechanisms for financing coral reef conservation in areas where use is currently high, or potentially high enough to generate adequate revenues at a fee level which users are willing to pay. This situation exists throughout the insular

Caribbean and in many other tropical countries. However, the success of such mechanisms depends on a high level of public/private sector collaboration, on institutional arrangements which allow for the revenue collected to be earmarked specifically for management of the resources, and on flexible fund-raising strategies which include other mechanisms to assure adequate levels of management during periods of low visitation or economic downturns. In areas where user fees are not an option, other less direct approaches must be considered.

Marine Eco-Tourism: Fundamental Characteristics and Links to Conservation

Tundi Agardy
World Wildlife Fund

Nature-based tourism that occurs in coastal areas, commonly called marine eco-tourism, can provide economic and social incentives for promoting coral reef conservation. However, development of tourism in coastal areas of developing countries can be fraught with risk, and those looking to eco-tourism as a way of supporting and financing conservation must evaluate local conditions and constraints carefully. Planners, prospective participants, and financiers of eco-tourism development must consider the social and cultural dimensions, the ecological and environmental dimensions, and the long term economic feasibility before reaching conclusions about the suitability of eco-tourism development in an area.

Eco-tourism can benefit conservation in at least two major ways. Outside attention on the value of the reef resource can spark both local and national interest in protecting it, opening the door for marine protected areas, coastal management plans, and effective resource management. In addition, revenues generated from tourism can be used to finance conservation projects and management, in the form of monitoring and enforcing regulations, establishing permit systems, constructing mooring buoys, and the like. The link between development and conservation runs in the other direction as well–such that effective conservation can be a significant "draw" for eco-tourism.

Although most might think otherwise, marine eco-tourism comprises more than scuba diving-based recreation. In the coral reef context, eco-tourism activities include diving and snorkeling, swimming and boating, "seascape" viewing and amateur collecting. These are tourism activities that utilize coral reef resources directly. Less direct are tourism activities that depend on the existence of a healthy intact reef system, even when tourists do not come into contact with the reef itself. Such tourism includes some forms of beach tourism, cultural or anthropological tourism, scientific tourism, and landscape viewing more generally. Development that can capitalize on a diversity of visitor interests, and therefore take some pressure off the primary target resource, may in some cases be more sustainable than simple dive tourism.

There are, however, costs associated with tourism development, even when it is eco-tourism (and therefore thought to be ecologically and socially sensitive). Some of these costs include the impacts brought about by greater access to ocean space and greater demand for resources, higher local population densities and internal migration to the coastal area, cultural contamination and undermining of traditional power structures, and a movement toward resource specialization that may counter efforts for broader biodiversity conservation. Furthermore, the price of success of even small-scale eco-tourism can be to unleash demands for ever-larger scales of tourism development. Keeping nature-based tourism from running amuck and developing into wholly unsustainable mass tourism is the challenge that confronts all those interested in exploring the links between eco-tourism and conservation.

What are possible safeguards against such out-of-control tourism development? From an ecological perspective, assessments need to be made concerning the carrying capacity of the environment for tourism use, including infrastructure, services to the tourist industry, direct reef exploitation, and indirect degradation brought about by a suite of cumulative pressures on the resource base. This carrying capacity should be re-evaluated periodically as conditions and demands change. From a sociological perspective, the tourism activity proposed should be evaluated for its suitability and potential risk to local societies. And involving local stakeholders, as early as possible in the planning process, is perhaps the most important step that can be taken to ensure that eco-tourism development is sustainable over the long run.

Environmental Trust Funds

Barry Spergel
World Wildlife Fund

Environmental trust funds are an innovative financing mechanism being used by more than twenty countries to cover the recurrent costs of conservation activities, such as strengthening environmental institutions, conserving biological diversity, and promoting sustainable development in general. [1] Environmental funds are established as independent legal entities outside of government, and are managed by a board of directors within the country concerned. An environmental fund acts as an in-country donor that awards grants to NGOs, government agencies and local community groups. For example, an environmental fund in Uganda allocates 60 percent of its grants for projects in local communities surrounding the national parks, 20 percent for park management, and 20 percent for research activities.

Usually an environmental fund is set up with an endowment from international donors, and then invested to produce a steady stream of income for supporting conservation activities. These endowments vary in size from US$1-100 million or more. Money for the endowment may come from grants by international aid donors, private sector sources, and often from debt-for-nature swaps or official debt forgiveness. Annual investment income from the endowment can be supplemented by revenues raised on an on-going basis from "conservation fees" or earmarked taxes collected from tourists and other natural resource "users."

Belize's Protected Area Conservation Trust is one example of an environmental fund which will be used to support coral reef conservation. The Trust will be funded by grants from international donors (creating an endowment), and by an $8 "conservation fee" charged to all foreign tourists entering the country (which will create a revolving fund). WWF has worked with Belize's Solicitor General to draft legislation to establish the fund by the end of 1995. The Trust will be governed by a Board of Directors with three NGO representatives, three government representatives (from the Ministry of Tourism and Environment; the Ministry of Natural Resources; and the Ministry of Agriculture and Fisheries), and two non-voting members (the Minister of Finance, and the executive director of the fund). There will also be an 11 member Advisory Council which will include representatives from the Ministry of Economic Development, the Ministry of Social Services, local governments, and NGOs not represented on the Board of Directors. The moneys raised by the Trust will be used to pay for hiring

---

[1] Environmental funds can be set up either as trust funds or foundations, depending on whether a country has a common law or civil law system. WWF has been involved in the design and establishment of thirteen environmental funds, four of which have been associated with the GEF.

extra park guards, training, protected area management, educational and public awareness programs and integrated conservation and development projects (particularly eco-tourism). Spending priorities will be determined on the basis of a five-year National Protected Recovery Plan approved by Cabinet.

Environmental funds vary from country to country in their structure, objectives, and financing mechanisms. Some have a focus on specific parks, or narrowly defined activities, while others have a broad conservation mandate. Most funds are set up in perpetuity, but some are designed to use up their endowment over a fixed period such as twenty years. But they all share some common features:

- Environmental funds aim to improve program stability, long-range planning, training and recruitment of personnel, by providing long-term funding security, and an institutional mechanism for stakeholders to work together on an ongoing basis.

- They generally have a board of directors composed of representatives from government agencies, local NGOs, scientific and technical experts, and representatives from local business groups and outside aid donors.

- The board of directors is guided and restricted in its choice of what projects and activities to fund by the terms of the charter or other legal document establishing the trust fund. This provides assurance to donors that the money which they contribute to a trust fund will only be used for stated purposes.

Two of the most important decisions in establishing a trust fund are determining the composition and voting structure of the board of directors, and securing agreement on what types of projects and activities can be funded.

Environmental funds can be particularly useful as a way to fund small-scale innovative projects and to provide a long-term secure source of funding for recurrent costs. However, environmental funds cannot and should not replace existing government expenditures for conservation. Core costs of staffing and park maintenance will always be a government's responsibility. Conversely, most developing country governments will only approve the creation of an independent off-budget fund if it will attract additional new revenues from either international donors, or tourist taxes and user fees.

There is an "opportunity cost" to tying up capital in an endowment: to provide annual income it has to stay in the bank or in other investments, and not be spent on today's needs. Whether this is worthwhile depends on spending needs, and financial insecurity, of the future compared to the need for extra funds today.

Global Environment Facility Trust Funds in Support of Conservation

Kathy Mikitin, Environment Department
World Bank

There are 12 conservation funds receiving or about to receive assistance from the GEF-Bank, either for design of a trust fund, a capital contribution or strengthening of an existing fund. Four of these funds are operational: Bhutan ($10 million), Peru ($4 million), Uganda ($5 million) and the Eastern Carpathian (Poland, Slovak, Ukraine for $0.6 million). The Seychelles Island Fund is receiving support to strengthen research and other scientific endeavors. While there are no funds that target marine protection per se, this is certainly a possibility either as the direct beneficiary of a trust fund or as part of a trust fund benefiting a national park system.

The basic legal concept behind a trust device is that property is managed by one person or group (usually referred to as "trustee(s)") for the identified goals or benefit of a second person or group (usually referred to as "beneficiary(ies)"). In GEF trust funds, the beneficiaries can be as abstract as forests and their surrounding communities, as is the case with the Uganda Mgahinga/Bwindi Forest Conservation Trust.

In general, GEF trusts are created with GEF and other donor funds set aside in perpetuity. These funds operate as endowments, with the net income generated from investing the trust assets serving to finance the recurrent costs, community support, research and other expenditures necessary to sustaining conservation areas. These funds are managed by boards of directors, usually with a majority of nongovernment representatives (that is, NGO, private sector, donors) comprising the board membership. The Board is obligated to follow a number of legal and administrative instruments (for example, trust deed, by-laws, trust administrative manual) which are reviewed by the Bank before releasing any capital contribution to the trust fund. The trust capital or assets are in most cases held offshore and managed by an investment firm.

GEF trust funds for biodiversity conservation are not free-standing mechanisms. All are designed in conjunction with or as a subsequent stage of investment in the creation, reform or upgrading of conservation areas, systems or institutions. The trust fund is intended to sustain activities or actions already underway. Most have been designed to provide long term, sustained financing to meet recurrent costs of operating and maintaining protected areas or to ensure sustainable use of natural resources through community support.

This type of trust fund has increasing appeal because of its obvious potential to stabilize the flow of resources to meet the long term recurrent costs of conservation initiatives. However seductive the option may be to the conservation planner, GEF-supported trust funds are not a panacea and should be chosen only after all other, and often simpler, means of securing recurrent cost financing have been examined and deemed infeasible or inappropriate.

The disadvantages of conservation trust funds must also be considered. Trust funds which seek to meet recurrent costs from net income while maintaining the value of their assets in real terms in perpetuity are subject to complex financial and administrative arrangements. Furthermore, there is an opportunity cost of tying up the substantial capital required to generate very small amounts of net income.

Knowing when the high "price" of a trust fund needs to be paid is important; hence, lower cost, equally sustainable alternative solutions deserve close review. Possible alternatives include a political commitment by governments to long-term recurrent budget support, establishing user-charges consistent with demand and carrying capacity for the ecosystems under use, extracting resource rents for conservation, creating stable long-term programs of donor assistance and using variations on conventional trust funds.

The Bank has also joined other institutions among which are UNDP, IUCN, WWF, TNC, CI, the Inter-American Development Bank, USAID, the Smithsonian, MacArthur and Mott Foundations in an informal coalition to further the use of conservation funds. The joint effort is aimed at expanding donor participation and contributions to conservation funds and at promoting interaction between the various existing and newly developing funds so that all may learn from experience.

Global Environment Facility

Kathy Mackinnon, Environment Department
World Bank

Guidance from the Conference of the Parties (COP) and the biodiversity operational strategy for the GEF Council will help to promote conservation of marine resources. Projects that qualify for GEF assistance under the convention have to be national priorities for any country wishing to submit GEF proposals for funding.

Priorities include:

- Identification and monitoring of biodiversity (that is, inventory projects)
- Capacity building
- Facilitating access to technology that promotes conservation and sustainable use of biodiversity
- Promoting sustainability (financial or otherwise).

The COP requested that innovative measures be sought, including economic incentives, projects that strengthen local and indigenous peoples' involvement, projects that focus on conservation management, projects that promote conservation and sustainable use of endemic species, and sustainable use of ecosystems, with marine and coastal ecosystems being specifically mentioned.

Any country wishing to propose a project must have ratified the biodiversity convention. This applies to a developing country or an economy in transition. The GEF asks that a project be a national priority within some kind of national strategic framework (that is, a biodiversity action plan, or a national environmental action plan).

In the GEF pilot phase, the portfolio was remarkably lacking in marine and coastal projects. One reason is that countries are looking landward, and do not often propose such projects. In the World Bank portfolio there is only one marine biodiversity project, but we are hoping for more in the future. COP is placing an emphasis on marine conservation projects, and it is expected to be discussed during the next COP meeting in November.

GEF projects are looking for local ownership and local involvement at all levels–from government down to local communities and NGOs. The GEF is also looking for partnerships between government agencies and the private sector, NGOs and local communities, for both implementation and funding.

GEF is also considering an early rewards system–some mechanism to reward local communities for initiatives they take to promote conservation. This system would apply to marine or terrestrial cases. GEF specifically asks that projects address the issue of financial sustainability–trust funds, sinking funds, user fees, alternative livelihood opportunities. There is a hope, although not an expectation, that many GEF projects will be sustainable financially by the end of the project term (for example, 5 to 7 years). This is not always a realistic hope, but almost all GEF projects are looking for ways in which to address the issue of financial sustainability.

All projects must have capacity building as a component, and all projects have to address the issue of incremental costs (that is, the GEF will only pick up those costs over and above what could reasonably be expected to be spent by governments if there were no GEF project).

As a final point, the secretariat is interested in opportunities for co-financing. The GEF has recently prepared a biodiversity operational strategy, which deals specifically with three areas:

- Enabling activities-helping countries with biodiversity strategies and action plans
- Short-term programs and projects (that is, opportunities that are too good to miss)
- Long-term programs (operational programs with a specific theme).

Particular emphasis is placed on coastal and marine programs and protected areas.

Although the biodiversity operational strategy gives the opportunity for spreading resources across all ecosystems, there will be a special emphasis on areas with species richness and high endemism. Thus, the tropics are particularly likely to benefit.

Comments

1. With respect to eco-tourism: a) eco-tourism is destined to run amuck; b) the pitfalls are much larger than the benefits in the long run; c) a tourist tax is probably more profitable and able to avoid pitfalls; and d) debt-for-nature swaps have been subjected to pressure (directly and indirectly) from structural adjustment programs. The World Summit for Social Development held in Copenhagen in March, 1995 had innovative language with respect to insulating social programs from structural adjustment pressures. Could there be a way to tie debt-for-nature swaps with debt-for-social development swaps?

2. There does seem to be willingness to pay among tourists, but a lack of willingness to charge. What can we do collectively to convince the waterfront community that it is not a bad thing?

3. The GEF is concentrating on national priorities, but is there opportunity to support regional interest (that is, several countries getting together and proposing a project) for GEF support? Is there any part of GEF available for this?

4. We are in a very critical juncture in the development of the GEF operational strategy. At this point, the draft does not appear to be realistic on the issue of financial sustainability for biodiversity or international waters projects. In part this is because there is a drum beat from the providers of GEF financing to minimize the amount of financing that goes into individual projects–to spread it as widely as possible, and rigorously expect this incremental cost condition. The result is a constant drum beat of pressure to try and design projects that are inherently financially sustainable–or go a long way toward achieving sustainability. Now in the case of coral reef conservation projects, this is ridiculously unrealistic–they are talking about five-year projects. As we heard earlier, even in the more developed areas with considerable tourism potential, we're talking about 10-15 years to achieve financial sustainability built into projects. We have to make sure that the GEF operational strategy recognizes this problem.

Panel Responses

1. (Barry Spergel). Debt forgiveness: I would reiterate that most of the environmental trust funds have devoted a good part of their resources to local communities that derive economic benefits from being near MPAs (for example, programs like the CAMPFIRE program, to more direct types of subsidies for increased social and health care services).

With respect to the question on willingness to charge, I think there needs to be a certain political change in countries. What has been tried in a number of different places has been charging different fees for different categories of visitors, or different fees for different types of parks. For example, in [the U.S.] one might imagine a $20-30 fee for the "crown jewel" parks (that is, Yosemite, Yellowstone National Park) and possibly a lower fee for smaller parks, such as Great Falls [Washington, D.C.].

The reason why these have not worked in the past is that the money often goes into general revenues, and is not earmarked for the parks. This affects the willingness to pay. We have done a number of marketing studies in Belize and Namibia which have found that if tourists know that the money will be earmarked specifically for conservation activities, they are willing to pay hundreds of dollars extra.

2. (Tighe Geoghegan). Phase One of implementing the Bonaire Marine Park is a classic example of the reluctance to charge on the part of the commercial users, and in every single case in the Caribbean the commercial users have, at first, resisted the implementation of user fees. In every single case the key to overcoming this has been to initiate a planning process both for the development of the revenue generation strategy and for the management of the protected area that fully incorporated those users. And in every case, when the users started to see that they would be involved and consulted in management decisions, suddenly it was very much in their interest to assist in implementing user fees. In the case of Bonaire, the commercial users were not initially consulted and reacted angrily. In Saba, while they were consulted in the initial stages of the system, a unilateral decision was taken by management to double the fee, and they resisted at that point. Thus, if serious management partnership (and not token ones) and if the users are consulted on implementation, they come up with innovative ideas and are willing to implement. However, this is a long process, and requires a sincere effort in consensus building and participatory planning.

3. (Kathy Mackinnon). At the moment, there is no specific percentage of resources allocated to regional programs. There are regional programs in the south Pacific and eastern Caribbean. The advantage of a regional program is that it may cover more than one GEF focal area (that is, biodiversity and international waters). However, even within the context of regional programs it is helpful if what the countries want to do have been identified as national priorities–the countries have to want to undertake a regional program, and very often they do if they see it as an extra opportunity, but may not want to if they think it is their only opportunity for GEF resources. For small island states it makes extremely good sense for them to have a regional program. If there is a proposal put

forward, each country involved would need to have individually ratified the Convention, otherwise it would not be considered.

4. (Barry Spergel). One solution that has been tried (in the Great Barrier Reef), that could be an answer, is very careful zoning of uses. If uses, such as mass tourism, are focused in areas that are not biologically unique, low entrance fees can be charged. In unique areas, where low impact is desired, charging high user fees will aim for the top of the market.

5. (John Dixon). Three observations were particularly noteworthy:

- There are opportunities for revenue generation and sustainable financing, both from the individual level (that is, users fees) to the level of trust funds, where a marine protected area is fortunate enough to receive money that can be managed to provide ongoing, sustainable support.

- Partnerships exist between private users, user groups, local communities and governments. All four are very important dimensions.

- There may be potential benefits to limiting or removing the role of governments from resource management. Problems identified include an inability or unwillingness of government to earmark funds specifically for a given protected area. Willingness to pay has been observed as closely tied with a distrust in government spending. Also, in many cases, governments have been inefficient in the delivery of goods and services for conservation.

III. Income-Generating Opportunities and Environmental Limitations

Introduction

Louise Scura, Environment Department
World Bank

Natural resources in and around coral reefs have the potential to economically benefit local communities and nations in areas such as fisheries (commercial and subsistence), recreation and tourism, pharmaceuticals, and perhaps in other ways, provided that uses are sustainable. This session continues the previous theme of sustaining coral reef conservation through financing by addressing a series of related issues including: mechanisms for revenue generation; cost-effective remediation of problems affecting reefs; and management frameworks to help strike a balance between different and possibly conflicting reef uses.

The panelists in this session have varied backgrounds ranging from business and resource management, to chemistry and quantitative ecology. The topics discussed could easily constitute full-day workshops by themselves; but hopefully, this session will provide several examples of the range of opportunities and issues.

The first presentation, by David Newman, addresses actual and potential markets as sources of revenue through resource extraction. The two following presentations by John Walch and Walter Adey examine potential benefits through alternative technology and reduced costs of community infrastructure by use of pollution abatement and resource recycling. The presentation by Billy Causey provides examples of resource management that recognize the limitations of coral reefs and associated systems, and suggest options through application of technology and multiple-use forms of zoning. Finally, the presentation by Ricardo Meléndez describes the importance of conflict resolution and equitable benefit sharing to the sustainability of conservation efforts.

Marine Bioprospecting

David Newman, Natural Products Branch
Developmental Therapeutics Program
National Cancer Institute

"Bioprospecting"–what is meant by this term?[1] In today's lexicon, it implies the search for an economically viable product that is found in a directed search of the planet's biological diversity using some form of activity filter. This brief summary addresses the search of a portion of the earth's marine biodiversity for chemical entities that may lead to new drug agents against the twin scourges of cancer and AIDS.

For the last thirty-five years, the U.S. National Cancer Institute has supported a program that has searched the earth's biodiversity (that is, decades before the term was first used) for chemical structures that might have utility as anti-cancer agents. Examples are the podophyllotoxins, camptothecins and taxol (all from terrestrial plant sources) that are now part of the physician's armamentarium, and many others that made it only part of the way along the very harsh road from discovery to commercialized drug.

Coral Reefs as Sources of Pharmacophores

The coral reef may well be considered the rain forest of the marine environment. Within this unusual microcosm, there is a very tightly interrelated environment, with many genera of invertebrate organisms conducting what is effectively chemical warfare just to keep a foothold on the reef so that they and their offspring might survive and reproduce in the harsh marine environment. As a result of this interminable warfare, very specialized chemical agents have been developed by individual species so that they will not become prey for other organisms. Think for a moment about the defenses that an individual marine invertebrate might have. A hard shell; a glue-like excretion; an outer hard surface. What might one have, however, if you are a shell-less mollusk, brightly colored and fleshy, and very slow moving? Wouldn't such an organism be a prime tidbit for something higher up the food chain? Amazingly, these organisms survive and reproduce. It turns out that most of them contain very potent toxins against those organisms that would normally desire them.

With the advent of SCUBA techniques, the chemist and pharmacologist began to investigate the marine environment as a source of pharmaceutical agents, much

---

[1] For a copy of the Letter of Intent, slides used in the presentation, or for further information on NCI's marine collection program, contact the author at the address and numbers in the appendix.

in the manner that forest and jungle dwellers have done for millennia with plants. In the last twenty-five years or so, an ever increasing number of novel chemical compounds have been reported in the scientific literature. Initially, these were simply of the genre, "I have found these interesting chemicals in such and such an organism." These could be considered to be the marine equivalent of the multifarious reports of interesting chemicals produced by such and such a plant. In the last twenty years the emphasis in marine chemistry has moved from the, "Look what a novel structure," "Look what an interesting biological activity from this chemical." This has been driven by a few essential factors, including a realization of the distinctly different chemistry in the marine environment, the rise of rapid testing systems that require only small amounts of crude active samples, the money to be made if one finds a novel pharmaceutical agent and the inquisitiveness of scientists in general. Unlike the corresponding studies in the terrestrial sphere, there is a paucity of anecdotal information as to medicinal efficacy of marine invertebrates. Contrasted with the information about medicinal plants in Asian communities one can appreciate the necessity for biologists and chemists to work together in the discovery of novel agents.

This raises perhaps the most important point. In all bioprospecting, and particularly in the marine bioprospecting arena, it is absolutely essential that the materials be assayed in as many different types of biological/biochemical tests as possible. This maximizes the possibilities of discovering an economically viable agent from a given organism.

It should be emphasized that "bioprospecting" is not the "silver bullet" that will convert a dying coral reef (or any other ecological niche) into a viable prospect; many NGOs, for-profits and even central governments have fallen into this trap.

Pharmaceutical Potential: Pros and Cons

In terms of pharmaceutical potential, there are two positive aspects to such a search:

1. Very high potential return if successful
2. Many potential markets (diseases) to conquer.

On the less positive side, there are at least four major concerns:

1. Time frame from discovery to drug measured in many years (7-20)
2. Initial value of an untested random sample is very low ($10 or less)
3. Odds of any one sample in any one screen making it to market ≤ 1 to 250,000
4. Cost of collection, processing and initial testing can be high.

However, it should also be borne in mind that the costs associated with the testing of synthetic chemical compounds are equivalent, as are the odds of success.

Since 1987, NCI has collected over 8,000 kilogram samples of shallow water marine invertebrates, mainly from the Central and South Pacific Ocean areas. These are deep frozen within two to five hours of collection (samples are kept in aerated seawater until frozen) and subsequently shipped to Frederick, MD for processing, testing, assay and storage. Approximate per sample costs are as follows:

Collection:	1 kg sample (frozen at site and maintained frozen)	$500+
Processing:	preparation of aqueous and organic extracts, storage	$150+
Initial testing:	*in vitro* 60 cell line anti-tumor screen	$200+
	in vitro live HIV screen	$150+
Further testing:	*in vitro* and *in vivo* preclinical pharmacology.	$100K+
	(for selected materials)	

From these figures, which are at the low end, one can see the level of financing and infrastructure needed before the pharmaceutical potential of any one sample can be evaluated. Obviously, the more screens in which a given material can be tested, the better the odds of a hit and the greater the probability of a commercial success. However, the odds of a commercial product from any one sample do not seem to drop below about 1 in 80,000 irrespective of the different assays in which it is tested.

Protection of Producers, Genetic Resources and Intellectual Property Rights

An explicit part of the NCI's collection program and one that is to be recommended to all groups that intend to perform such operations, is to make sure that the intellectual property rights (IPR) of the producing country (government and scientists) are protected prior to collections commencing. NCI has established a Letter of Collection (LOC), that we use as the basis for a collection agreement with the governments (or other legal permitting entities) in the producing countries. This document spells out the conditions under which we collect, the safeguards for IPR and contains the requirement that if any organization wishes to license a material for further development, then that organization must involve the producing country in the licensing procedures. A copy of this document is freely available from the author and may be used by organizations as a model. This protocol has been used as the basis for collection and screening agreements with a variety of producing countries across the globe over the last few years.

  SUSTAINABLE FINANCING MECHANISMS FOR CORAL REEF CONSERVATION

Even in the cases of countries from whom we have valid collection permits but no formal agreement, we insist that our contract collectors (currently The Coral Reef Research Foundation based in Chuuk Atoll, Federated States of Micronesia) adhere to the tenets of the LOC and we will also adhere to these tenets in any further development of an active hit. These include that information will be sent back to the producing countries and that all collections, be they initial or recollections, are made with a proper regard for ecological disruptions that might occur in the process.

Examples of Successful Bioprospecting Forays

There are a number of materials that are in clinical trials, or are in the pipeline undergoing early to late preclinical studies, that may in time produce a viable drug candidate. They include Manoalide and derivatives (a potential anti-inflammatory compound) from the sponge, *Luffariella variabilis*, Pseudopterosin E from the gorgonian, *Pseudopterogorgia elisabethae*, another anti-inflammatory, Bryostatin 1 from the bryozoan, *Bugula neritina* (Phase II cancer trials in the U.S.) and Dolastatin 10 from the mollusk, *Dolabella auricularia* (entering Phase I cancer trials in the U.S.) to materials such as Halomon from the rhodophyte, *Portieria hornemannii*, Ecteinascidin from the tunicate, *Ecteinascidia turbinata* and Halichondrin B, from the as yet unspeciated sponge, *Lissodendoryx* sp.; the last three are all in various stages of preclinical development.

Large Scale Recollections: A Problem Area

In the preceding discussion with the exception of the examples above, the initial collection of material has been for the discovery phase. With the discovery of an interesting activity, comes the daunting realization that one will have to recollect large quantities of an organism to obtain enough material for further experiments, and the more successful the compound, the more material required. This is an area to which NCI has given a lot of thought and often been pioneers.

Thus, in the case of bryostatin, it was necessary to collect 38,000 kilograms of the bryozoan to produce 18 grams of compound for clinical trials. This was done in an ecologically sensitive manner off Palos Verdes, California, and at the same time, NCI funded successful aquacultural work on the production of the tunicate [and the metabolite] in a closed cycle land based program with CalBioMarine Technologies. In the case of the halichondrin producer, *Lissodendoryx*, in conjunction with the New Zealand government, NCI funded a recollection ecological study of the sponge bed at 100+ m, and then in a joint 50:50 manner, funded in-sea aquaculture of this organism at 10 to 30 m, where the sponge is growing well and producing the required compounds. In addition to this, we also have funded a 1 ton deep water recollection with the express consent of the New Zealand government, to obtain enough biomass to purify 400 milligrams of the metabolite for further preclinical studies.

Export and Import of Materials

It is absolutely essential that the producing country's permitting authorities be involved in both the initial and subsequent collection. Although frequently there is permission granted by an in-country NGO or by a University collaborator in the producing country, such permission is not in line with the U.N. Convention on Biological Diversity, which requires the permission of the appropriate source country government agency, and it is of little value as a bargaining chip when one is held at the port of exit for illegal export of genetic resources. One must also be aware of the regulations (that is, U.S. Dept. of Agriculture; U.S. Fish and Wildlife Service) as importation of foreign-sourced raw materials into the United States and its movement within the USA is very tightly controlled for obvious reasons. Finally, no reputable commercial operation will license the rights to a compound unless the provenance of the material is unquestionable.

Final Comments

The coral reef is a wondrous source of both beauty and of potential pharmacophores. It should be approached with the aim of maximizing its genetic diversity and potential but without destroying this fragile ecosystem. As stated in the above discussion, the "search for a silver bullet" from the reef is long, arduous and expensive in both money and time; however, the potential returns are also vast if one produces a viable economic entity. Even if no final product comes from a search, if the operation is conducted correctly, a significant amount of important scientific information is obtained and disseminated, leading to a greater understanding of the coral reef ecosystem.

Opportunities in Sustainable Mariculture

John Walch
SeaPhix, L.L.C.

SeaPhix, L.L.C. is associated with the marine aquarium industry, an industry often implicated in the destruction of coral reefs and the collection of its inhabitants. However, SeaPhix is involved in the propagation, and not collection, of ornamental marine-life. SeaPhix is motivated by the initiative of a private enterprise to reduce or possibly eliminate the destruction of coral reef habitats and the collection of its inhabitants for ornamental reasons. Another goal for SeaPhix is to assure that the educational benefits derived from maintaining an enclosed marine environment continues to be available for future generations.

The world's present social/ecological paradigm is evolving–from one that used to encourage collectors of caterpillars, placing them in jars only to have them die, to one that now motivates children to place a caterpillar in a terrarium and enjoy watching it metamorphose into a butterfly and released into nature. The marine aquarium hobby is also evolving–from the days of bleached coral skeletons, which decorated a sterile, malnourished fish tank, to one that now maintains a total marine ecosystem with reproducing live corals and healthy fish.

Advancements in filtration methods and an increased awareness of the complex requirements of marine-life have inspired the marine aquarium trade to make some drastic changes over the past few years. A diligent effort by aquarists to purchase cultured marine-life (when available), self imposed "green labeling," and growth in aquarium societies, like the Marine Aquarium Conference of North America and the Southwest Marine Conference, indicate an alternative conservation movement.

Cultured ornamental marine life is a relatively new concept and one that is well received by consumers and encouraged by government regulatory agencies. SeaPhix has structured its entire business and products around this concept and offers assistance in all phases.

Our equipment (insulated larval rearing tanks, spawning towers, juvenile fish grow-out tanks, daylight spectrum lights, lunar lighting, Algal Turf Scrubber™ filter boxes, non-traumatic pumps) are included in ecoReef 6000™ mariculture installations and were designed for an exact, and unique, application. This patented equipment was created for the propagation of ornamental marine life based on a total ecosystem approach. The equipment and applied technology enables commercial scale propagation without the need of water changes, costly mechanical and chemical filtration or the need to be located next to non-polluted saltwater. The equipment is also combined in such a manner to allow it to fit in a small building. This building can be located near or directly within the marketplace.

SeaPhix is currently installing commercial scale mariculture facilities within metropolitan "pocket market" locations. The first is already in operation in Tennessee, while the second, located in Indiana, is being completed and should be producing by the fall of 1995. These revolutionary culture systems have the ability to produce tons of "live-rock" annually.

Live-rock is the calcium carbonate rock which creates the backbone of coral reefs. This is also the main ingredient used in the "reef" aquarium trade, and is collected from the world's reefs at alarming rates. While we encourage the production of live-rock within our mariculture systems, it is a secondary product, with the main products being live corals and ornamental reef fishes. By creating a mesocosm within our culture systems, a habitat develops which encourages rapid growth and the sexual and asexual propagation of both hard and soft corals. This total ecosystem approach also produces natural conditions, including the presence of life sustaining plankton required for the propagation of numerous reef species.

The same natural filtration methods and non-traumatic pump design that is used within our research and commercial production facilities has now been successfully adapted into the *ecoTarium*. This hobbyist-scale marine aquarium drastically reduces the mortality of corals and fish by providing a much more stable and healthy environment, at the same time provides the owner a less labor intensive system.

Market Expansion

However, these facilities are not Seaphix's only commercial opportunity. During the company's preliminary research, SeaPhix learned how certain corals and reef-fish species reproduce and that some are well suited to commercial propagation within our systems. We have also discovered that certain species experience high mortalities during the long shipping time associated with the distance between the collection point and the market, but because of their popularity in the aquarium trade, they continue to be shipped. SeaPhix plans to economically culture as many of these species as possible within our systems. However, the company will continue research on new species and add to the already sizable list of successfully cultured ones.

Throughout our research SeaPhix has learned that some corals and fish require extended time periods or unique surroundings to reach market maturity, making them economically unfavorable. The reproductive technology gained from these species can be transferred to natural coastal mariculture operations better suited for their commercial-scale propagation. This strategic alliance between SeaPhix and foreign mariculture facilities will enable us to offer a greater diversity of cultured organisms and become more competitive with marine collectors. Since our intention is to drastically reduce the need to collect ornamental marine-life from the reef, we will be affecting the employment of people who earn a living collecting, packing, and shipping this product. By forming our alliance with countries already involved in the industry we utilize the present skilled labor force and established infrastructure, and offer potential alternative employment to the people who once earned a living through collecting. SeaPhix will provide not only the original technology needed, but will continue to offer technical support and serve as the marketing arm of these win/win relationships.

A generic example might proceed as follows:

An existing mariculture facility which is currently producing edible seafood may want to expand into ornamental marine life, or a government or private sector with a mariculture site (for example, a marine protected area) may want to start culturing ornamental marine life. SeaPhix provides a site selection feasibility study and makes recommendations as to what species are best suited for culturing. SeaPhix also provides technology to culture the selected organisms on a commercial scale and provides a business plan outlining the profit potential.

Once the facility is producing, SeaPhix can provide the marketing outlet for the cultured products through our retail stores and direct mail order outlet. SeaPhix also provides training for proper and humane packaging and handling of the marine life, so it arrives at receiving stations in excellent condition.

Significant planning has already gone into this phase, including preliminary species selection, cost factors associated with air-freight, the ability to pay fair market value. SeaPhix is negotiating with interested mariculture operations located in the Solomon Islands and in the Caribbean and plan to establish strategic alliances by the end of 1995.

Maintaining an enclosed marine ecosystem is an excellent way of sharing the secrets of life on a coral reef. Children in contact with marine life have a heightened awareness of coral reefs and a general concern for the marine environment. Not everyone will have the means to travel to see coral reefs first hand, but exposure to the reef and other marine ecosystems in the classroom or in private homes may increase future generations' sensitivity to the need for protection of the world's reefs.

Cost-Effective Wastewater Remediation for the Protection of Coral Reef Environments

Walter Adey, Marine Systems Laboratory
Smithsonian Institution

Coral reef environments are highly oligotrophic. The addition of relatively small quantities of nutrients severely unbalances the dynamic relationships between freestanding algae, their grazers and stony corals, the primary providers of essential community structure. Agricultural run-off, domestic wastewaters and more recently aquacultural run-off, as failing wild fisheries are replaced by cultured production, have become increasingly serious destructive agents of coral reef ecosystems. Unfortunately, the highest quality tertiary wastewater treatment (the removal of nutrients), as currently practiced, is often prohibitively expensive, even in the strongest western economies. Capital costs of $15-25/gallon of daily capacity has been standard for the industry, and phosphorus, a particularly difficult contaminant, typically costs $0.50 to 1.50/gram to remove at an established wastewater facility.

Shallow water, high energy coral reefs are the most productive ecosystems on earth. Mean rates of production of 15 g (dry wgt)/m^2/day have been published, and well documented studies showing 25-50 g (dry wgt)/m^2/day, in favorable environments, have been carried out. This magnitude of primary production requires an extraordinary capability for the extraction of nitrogen and phosphorus from the overflowing oligotrophic waters and has long suggested a methodology for the remediation of wastewaters to tertiary levels.

The Marine Systems Laboratory, a living systems modeling group at the Smithsonian Institution, has developed techniques for adapting the capabilities of coral reef primary production to engineered systems. These have been extensively used for controlling water quality in model ecosystems from coral reefs to estuaries and fresh water streams. The process, generalized as algal turf scrubbing (ATS), has been commercialized and developed for the tertiary, quaternary and quinary treatment of domestic, agricultural, aquacultural and industrial wastewaters.

In tropical/subtropical environments, a solar driven, commercial scale, 1 million gpd, 5,000m^2 tertiary domestic wastewater ATS plant can produce algae at 50-70 g(dry)/m^2/day and remove nitrogen at 9 kg/day and phosphorous at 6 kg/day. This is a "low tech" facility that can be built and operated in most countries. The capital cost of current ATS plants built in the U.S. is about $1/gallon of daily capacity and will probably drop as more plants are constructed. Wastewater treatment involving microbial disinfection is considerably cheaper. The long term operational cost of the recovery of phosphorus in such a facility in the U.S. today is less than $0.03/gram, assuming that no value is applied to the removal of any other component. The high protein, nutrient rich, recyclable algal product has demonstrated value as both a plant fertilizer and an aquaculture feed for a commercially useful fish (*Tilapia*). At $0.15 to 0.25/equivalent dry lbs., operational costs of nutrient amelioration can be largely or totally recovered through developing an appropriate market for the product. In the central valley of California, ATS systems are currently being developed as a commercially viable source of water rights. This technology is ideal for application in tropical latitudes, and in arid and semiarid coral reef environments, where wastewater recovery can provide considerable economic incentive to nutrient amelioration.

An Ecosystem Approach to Managing Marine Protected Areas for Sustainable Use

Billy Causey
Florida Keys National Marine Sanctuary

The Florida Keys extend approximately 220 miles southwest from the southern tip of the Florida peninsula in the United States. Located adjacent to the Keys' land mass are spectacular, unique, and nationally significant marine environments, including seagrass meadows, mangrove islands, and extensive living coral reefs. These marine environments support rich biological communities and possess high value to human beings, such as conservation, recreational, commercial, ecological, historical, research, educational, and aesthetic values, all which give this area special national significance. These communities are the marine equivalent of tropical rain forests in that they support high levels of biological diversity, are fragile and easily susceptible to damage from human activities.

The lure of the Florida Keys–the clear tropical waters, bountiful resources, and appealing natural environment have been among the many fine qualities that attracted visitors to the Keys for decades. However, warning signs that the Keys' environment and natural resources were fragile, and not infinite, came early. In 1957, a group of conservationists and scientists held a conference at the Everglades National Park and discussed the demise of the coral reef resources in the Keys at the hands of those who were attracted there because of their beauty and uniqueness. The conference resulted in action that created the world's first underwater park, the John Pennekamp Coral Reef State Park, in 1960. However, in just a little over a decade following that park's establishment, a public outcry was sounded that cited pollution, over-harvesting, physical impacts, overuse, and use conflicts as continuing problems. These concerns continued to be voiced by environmentalists and scientists alike throughout the decades of the 1970s, 1980s and indeed, into the 1990s.

Other management efforts were undertaken to protect the coral reefs of the Florida Keys. The Key Largo National Marine Sanctuary was established in 1975 to protect 103 square nautical miles of coral reef habitat stretching along the reef tract from just north of Carysfort Lighthouse to south of Molasses Reef, offshore of the Upper Keys. In 1981, the 5.32 square nautical mile Looe Key National Marine Sanctuary was established to protect the popular Looe Key Reef, located off Big Pine Key in the Lower Keys. These two sanctuaries are intensively managed. The installation of mooring buoys to protect the reefs from anchor damage, as well as educational programs, research and monitoring programs, and various resource protection programs, including interpretive law enforcement, have been concentrated in these two marine protected areas. However, the health of the coral reef resources has been affected by land-based sources of pollution and nutrients. Managing these two sites has been like trying to manage islands in the middle of the ecosystem. Obviously, the major threats come from outside their delineated boundaries. To be successful in their management, an ecosystem approach is required.

In 1989, mounting threats to the health and ecological future of the coral reef ecosystem in the Florida Keys prompted the U.S. Congress to take action to protect this fragile natural resource. The threat of oil drilling in the mid- to late-1980s off the Florida Keys, combined with reports of deteriorating water quality throughout the region, occurred at the same time scientists were assessing the adverse affects of coral bleaching, the die-off of the long-spined urchin, loss of living coral cover on reefs, a major seagrass die-off, declines in reef fish populations, and the spread of coral diseases. These were topics of major scientific concern, and the focus of several scientific workshops, when three large ships ran aground on the coral reef tract within a brief 18 day period in the fall of 1989. Coincidental as it may seem, it was this final physical insult to the reef that prompted the U.S. Congress to take action to protect the coral reef ecosystem of the Florida Keys. Although most remember the ship groundings as having triggered Congressional action, it was in fact the cumulative events of environmental degradation, in conjunction with the physical impacts, that prompted Congressional response.

On November 16, 1990, President George Bush signed into law the Florida Keys National Marine Sanctuary and Protection Act (FKNMS ACT). The Act designated 2,800 square nautical miles of coastal waters off the Florida Keys as the Florida Keys National Marine Sanctuary. The Sanctuary boundary extends southward on the Atlantic Ocean side of the Keys from the north easternmost point of the Biscayne National Park along the approximate 300-foot isobath for over 200 nautical miles to the Dry Tortugas. From there it turns north and east encompassing a large portion of the Gulf of Mexico and Florida Bay where it adjoins the Everglades National Park. The landward boundary is the mean high water mark. The Key Largo and Looe Key National Marine Sanctuaries, the State Parks and Aquatic Preserves, and the Florida Keys Refuges of the U.S. Fish and Wildlife Service are encompassed by the Sanctuary; whereas the Everglades National Park, Biscayne National Park, and Dry Tortugas National Park are excluded from the boundary.

The passage of the Act immediately addressed two major concerns of Florida Keys residents. First, there was an instant prohibition on any oil drilling, including mineral and hydrocarbon leasing, exploration, development, or production within the Sanctuary. In addition, the legislation prohibited the operation of tank vessels (ships) greater than 50 meters in length in an internationally recognized *Area to Be Avoided* within the Sanctuary boundary.

Clearly, the greatest threat to the natural resources of the Keys and its economy has been the degradation of water quality over the past two decades. Where it was once considered an exception for underwater visibility to drop below 30 m (100 ft) during the 1970s; today, visibility exceeding 15 m (50 ft) is considered the exception on most reefs of the Lower Keys throughout the year. Commercial and recreational users of the Keys' resources, environmentalists, scientists, and resource managers all agree that the water quality of the Keys is in sharp decline and that commercial and recreationally important resources are extremely threatened. Reasons for the decline are believed to include lack of fresh water entering Florida Bay; nutrients from domestic wastewater such as shallow-well injection, cess pits and septic tanks; stormwater runoff containing heavy metals, fertilizers and insecticides; discharges from marinas and live-aboards; poor flushing of canals and embayments; build-up of organic debris along the shoreline; sedimentation; lack of hurricanes; and environmental changes associated with global climate change and sea-level rise.

Congress recognized the critical role of water quality in maintaining Sanctuary resources when it directed the Administrator of the Environmental Protection Agency, in conjunction with the Governor of the State of Florida and in consultation with the Secretary of Commerce, to develop a comprehensive Water Quality Protection Program for the Sanctuary.

The FKNMS ACT called for the Secretary of Commerce, in consultation with appropriate Federal, State, and local government authorities to develop a comprehensive management plan and implementing regulations to achieve protection and preservation of living and other resources of the Florida Keys marine environment. The ACT calls for the management plan to protect the resources of the Sanctuary by educating and interpreting for the public regarding the Florida Keys marine environment and to manage human uses of the Sanctuary that result in resource degradation.

Since approximately 65 percent of the FKNMS encompasses Florida State waters and numerous state and federal areas of jurisdiction overlap or lie adjacent to the FKNMS boundary, it is imperative that the planning process for the Sanctuary be an inter/intra-agency effort. Also, due to the high level and diversity of public utilization of the resources in the Florida Keys and the importance of tourism to the economy of the Keys, it is equally important that the public have a strong role in the development of the comprehensive management plan.

The Sanctuary Act calls for the public to be a part of the planning process, and that a Sanctuary Advisory Council (SAC) be established to aid in the development of the comprehensive management plan. A 22-member Advisory Council, selected by the Governor of Florida and the Secretary of Commerce, consists of members of various user groups; local, state, and federal agencies; scientists; educators; environmental groups; and private citizens. Over the course of the planning process, numerous public workshops have been held to get input from knowledgeable individuals on a wide range of topics that could be implemented in the management of the Sanctuary.

The draft management plan for the Sanctuary contains a draft zoning plan, which represents a major departure from the traditional management actions in Sanctuaries. The establishment of a "Core Area" surrounding the shallow reef habitat at Looe Key Reef has been the Sanctuary Program's only other attempt to protect Sanctuary resources using zoning. The Act mandates that the Sanctuary program "consider temporal and geographical zoning, to ensure protection of sanctuary resources." The zoning plan presented in this paper represents the climax of an extraordinary consensus building process between Sanctuary planners, the SAC, and the public. Five types of zones are proposed:

Wildlife Management Zones. These are zones established to manage and protect wildlife resources of the Sanctuary, including endangered or threatened species and their habitats. These zones, which complement the management needs of the U.S. Fish and Wildlife Refuges in the Keys, are comprised of only 26 Keys (out of over 1,700 in the Keys) that have been set aside for managing access by the public. Access to the various Keys differs in the plan, some are permanently closed, others are seasonally or only partially closed. Impact to the public has been kept to a minimum.

Replenishment Reserves. There are three of these zones that comprise slightly over 5 percent of the total area of the 2,800 square nautical mile Sanctuary. They are located in the vicinity of the Dry Tortugas, Western Sambo Reef (lower Keys), and Carysfort Lighthouse (upper Keys). These zones will protect and enhance biodiversity by providing natural spawning, nursery, or permanent residence areas to replenish species populations, particularly those not protected by fishery management plans. They will help protect ecosystem functions in contiguous habitats. These are no-take zones where no form of resource harvest will be allowed.

Sanctuary Preservation Areas. These zones comprise only 0.18 percent of the total Sanctuary area, and protect shallow, heavily used reefs by prohibiting the taking of organisms where highly concentrated visitor-use leads to resource degradation. The zones are designed to enhance the reproductive capabilities of renewable resources, protect areas critical for sustaining and protecting important marine species, and reduce user conflicts in high-use areas. There are 19 of these no-take areas distributed along the Atlantic side of the Keys.

Existing Management Zones. These zones will delineate the existing jurisdictional authority of other agencies (for example, state parks, aquatic preserves, wildlife refuges, sanctuaries, and other managed areas). These zones will recognize established management areas and facilitate management that complements existing programs in those areas, ensuring cooperation and coordination with other agencies.

Special-Use Zones. These zones are areas where specific issues will be addressed and special management programs (for example, monitoring, research, education, and restoration) can be conducted without impediment. They can be used to set aside areas for specific uses to reduce user conflicts and/or minimize the adverse environmental effects of high-impact activities. These zones will be established and limited by a period of time. There are four *research only* special-use zones proposed in this plan.

Zoning can be a useful management tool for marine protected areas, especially those as large as the Florida Keys National Marine Sanctuary. Zoning allows managers the perfect opportunity to balance resource use with resource protection, while keeping impact to the public at a minimum.

In recent years, the managers and scientists working in South Florida have recognized that the ecosystem is much larger than historically described. Where at Looe Key and Key Largo National Marine Sanctuaries we previously felt we were managing the coral reef, now we realize that these areas are only part of a larger ecosystem. Many of our management colleagues in South Florida also believed that within the boundaries of their jurisdiction they could effectively manage their sites. Today, managers and scientists working in South Florida see this as the geographical range of the South Florida ecosystem that must be managed as a single component. The ecosystem that we envision now begins at the headwaters of the Kissimmee River, includes Lake Okeechobee, the Everglades agricultural area, the Everglades, Florida Bay, through the Keys, and out to the reef tract. As a result of planning activities of the South Florida Ecosystem Restoration Task Force, established by Secretary of the Department of Interior Bruce Babbitt in 1993, a vision for the South Florida ecosystem has been developed and all agencies are working to implement restoration activities to re-establish the ecological and hydrological linkages of this larger ecosystem.

Another effort has been initiated by Governor Lawton Chiles, who has formed the Governor's Commission for a Sustainable South Florida. Many of the same agencies involved in the restoration efforts are also assisting in the development of a plan for a sustainable South Florida. The efforts of the South Florida Ecosystem Restoration Task Force and the Governor's Commission for a Sustainable South Florida, coupled with the comprehensive, integrated management planning for the Sanctuary will lead to protecting the marine resources of South Florida for the sustainable use of future generations.

Conflict Management and Benefit Sharing as a Means toward Conservation of Marine Biodiversity

Ricardo Meléndez
Fundación Futuro Latinoamericano

This paper summarizes a presentation of case studies related to the use of conflict management processes with the objective of attaining conservation of coastal and marine resources. Two cases are based on recent experiences fostered by Fundación Futuro Latinoamericano (FFLA).

Protection schemes, such as establishment of marine parks; funding mechanisms, such as duties and fees; and promotion of sound use of natural resources, such as diving and tourism, are necessary to promote the sustainability of fragile marine and coastal ecosystems. However, they might not be sufficient conditions for conserving marine resources, particularly in light of the impacts from land-based sources of pollution. Hence, the importance of working with the pertinent groups involved in these activities and the immediate stakeholders in the resources cannot be over-emphasized.

The Taura Syndrome

The Taura Syndrome is an unknown factor which fatally inhibits the growth of shrimp larvae. The Syndrome has detrimentally affected shrimp production, Ecuador's second most important export (excluding oil). Extensive research on the subject indicated, by May 1994, that the cause of the infection could possibly be pesticides used on the banana plantations which border the affected shrimp ponds in the same region along the coast of Ecuador. Bananas are Ecuador's most important export, as well as a critical employment sector. Both the banana plantations and the shrimp ponds depend on the waters of the Gulf of Guayaquil to sustain production. Several other sources of pollution, such as paper mills, rice plantations, gold mining and the country's largest human population, (the City-Port of Guayaquil) also occupy the same estuary. Contamination of the estuary has resulted in a heated conflict between the banana and shrimp industries, which escalated to national attention during the first quarter of 1995. The Guayas estuary is the largest on the Pacific coast in the Western Hemisphere and its waters have influence over marine and coastal areas vastly rich in biodiversity.

At the prompting of FFLA, a dialogue on the Taura Syndrome was convened in Guayaquil, Ecuador in July 1994, by the Minister of Agriculture and the Minister of Industry, Commerce and Fishing. Also attending were leaders from pertinent industrial sectors of the coast, as well as several other Latin American leaders who facilitated the discussions. The dialogue's two principal objectives were to agree on a definition of the problem, and to reach a consensus toward a means of resolution. The overall objective was to achieve the sustainable development of the Guayaquil estuary by means of participatory conflict management.

The result was the establishment of a Program for Sustainable Development of the Gulf of Guayaquil, later approved by the President of the Republic and, thus, institutionalized via the formation of a Joint Commission, involving government and private sector interests. Main stakeholders were engaged in finding solutions to the broader objective of sustainability and its implementation. Funds for supporting the activities will come from the Central Government and the private sectors involved.

Biodiversity

The Ecuadorian territory, both land and maritime, is rich in biodiversity. Concentrated over a relatively small surface area, its habitats, including tropical Pacific islands, coral reefs, mangroves, mountains, wetlands, and forests harbor among the world's highest concentration of species and genetic resources per square kilometer. Given the richness of Ecuadorian ecosystems, the management, understanding, and conservation of this unique heritage is of special interest to this country as well as to the world.

In May of 1995, a National Dialogue on Biodiversity and Sustainable Development was convened by the Secretary General of Planning, the President of the National Environmental Advisory Commission, and the Congressional Chair of the Environmental Commission, under the guidance of FFLA. Over the previous two years Ecuador had been involved in various trans-national agreements dealing with issues such as biodiversity, inter-Andean commerce, and intellectual property rights. However, lack of communication between the various participants of these conferences, as well as the limited understanding of biodiversity on a national level, led to the need for dialogue in 1995. The intent of the dialogue was to anticipate eventual conflicts that might arise between the numerous interest groups emerging, following the adoption and application of recent legislation. The more general objective was aimed as sustaining Ecuador's extraordinary biodiversity through participatory, decisionmaking processes and through legislative and normative development.

The result of the dialogue was manifold. On the national level there arose a greater recognition and understanding of biodiversity. Furthermore, various recommendations from the national dialogue have received congressional approval and been incorporated in national legislation. Finally, a greater communication and cooperation has been established between the many interest groups which are in some way affected by the issue of biodiversity.

Comment: (Graeme Kelleher). I would like to refer to a question asked by one of the panelists: "Was the Marine Protected Area program top-down?" The reason [the process] took four years was because it was basically bottom-up. The way we approached it was to create working groups in each of the regions, consisting of local managers and scientists, and they are the ones who made the recommendations and produced the reports. So if anyone got the impression that Australia dictated to the world what it should do, I can counter that allegation and state absolutely what happened is that Australia did what the rest of the world told it to do.

Question: To what extent could some of the pre-screening activities [for bioprospecting] could be done in-country with some training, so that value added to the actual marine organism, or active agent could be done at the country level?

Response: (David Newman). If the country has the necessary infrastructure (24-hour power, pure water), and the necessary funding to run the type of assay I described, yes; if not, then the answer is no. For example, we [National Cancer Institute] have a comparable program with plants and in Sarawak (part of Malaysia) a country representative was sent to NCI to learn the technology, and Sarawak has put enough money into building what is effectively a P-3 facility (that is, the ability to work with live agent). And this facility has 24-hour power. However, there are other assays that can be used in-country that are fairly unsophisticated, but are predictive. A major problem, however, is that if you get into extracting [marine organisms] you first have to get rid of the water. And to do this freeze drying is necessary–and this gets back to the problem: "Do you have 24-hour power?"

Question: In South Florida various uses of marine resources were mentioned. Do you feel that with the large number of visitors and the various revenues that are generated from different extractive and non-extractive uses that the prices are generally being set right, or, in talking about managing for sustainability and carrying capacity, are they too low?

Response: (Billy Causey). As far as the tourism and dive industries are concerned, I think they feel that they are right at the edge now, because they are competing with the Caribbean market. I think they feel reluctant to be the ones willing to charge the user fee–that this action may push them over the edge with their customers. For example, a customer originating in Chicago might consider a trip to the Caymans instead of the Florida Keys if user fees resulted in comparable prices. So it's teetering in some industries. We have a healthy commercial fishery market in some areas–unhealthy in others. We had a banner year for spiny lobster in 1995–the best in 20 years. The pink shrimp catch increased this year, so in the commercial fisheries, I think the situation is leveling out. The recreational fisheries are also doing well. I don't want to make it too glossy–there are problems. In the area of live rock harvesting we're seeing that phased out in the Keys, and we are encouraging people to go to mariculture.

Question. My name is DeeVon Quirolo and I am from Reef Relief. One of our strong issues has been to promote the development of a carrying capacity for the Florida Keys. Right now it has been relegated to an educational strategy, and I think it is a very important need that we have, because many of us feel we have exceeded the environmental carrying capacity in the Keys. What are your hopes for getting closer to a comprehensive carrying capacity [study] and how can you use the help of the NGO community to make that happen?

Response. (Billy Causey). I think we're going to have to tease out the environmental impacts to the resources from the anthropogenic impacts–both direct and secondary. Until the time in which we can do this, I do not believe that we are going to have the confidence of those that want to support sustainable use of the resources, but want hard numbers. That is the challenge that I hope I was able to present today, that if we get any financing, it is in looking at carrying capacity in different areas. As a multiple use program, we must avoid unduly restricting commercial and recreational activities. I think to arbitrarily pull those figures [carrying capacity] out of the air, would be counter to that mandate. But I want to manage on the conservative side, and I think [multiple-use] zoning gives us that option.

IV. Creating a Planning and Investment Framework through Partnerships

Introduction

John McManus
International Center for Living Aquatic Resources Management

This panel presents examples of partnerships developed at governmental, nongovernmental, and regional levels, along with private investment and local communities in efforts to establish and sustain marine protected areas and their conservation objectives. The panelists represent a broad range of experience and geographical coverage.

Large and Small-Scale Marine Protected Areas:
Planning, Investment and Intergenerational Quality of Life

John McManus
International Center for Living Aquatic Resources Management

Abstract

Two proposed marine protected areas in the South China Sea are contrasted in terms of planning and investment frameworks and their contributions to the intergenerational quality of life (IQL) of coastal villagers. The small (6 km^2) proposed marine reserve/park system in Bolinao, northwestern Luzon, is designed for bottom-up implementation and management within a coastal area planning and community development program. The proposed Spratly Island Marine Park involves 200,000 to 300,000 km^2 disputed by six claimant governments, and would require a top-down implementation and management by a professional organization. The two protected area systems are designed to provide sustainable harvests and other benefits to coastal villagers, in one case adjacent to the protected area, and in the other hundreds of miles away from it. The need is reiterated for setting aside 20 percent of all coral reef areas as small reserves and for a set of strategically placed larger reserves to ensure the maintenance of inter- and intra-specific biodiversity and IQL benefits to coastal dwellers.

A reasonable goal for the establishment of marine protected areas is the promotion of an equitable quality of life for affected people over several generations. This intergenerational quality of life (IQL) approach provides for both sustainable use and the maintenance of biodiversity as necessary preconditions to providing for the needs of future generations in the face of future uncertainties. There is a need to establish a clearly defined approach to evaluating positive and negative impacts to quality of life amid a variety of social contexts in which the definition of quality of life varies. However, a starting premise can rest on the acceptance of increasingly convergent international concepts of basic human needs.

This paper briefly discusses two marine protected areas which have been proposed, in Bolinao and the Spratly Islands respectively, and considers the planning and investment frameworks which will make them feasible and justifiable with regard to the IQL goal.

A Marine Reserve for Bolinao, Pangasinan

Bolinao is a town of approximately 50,000 people in western Luzon, Philippines. Nearly 20,000 people are dependent for livelihood on a fringing reef complex of about 100 km^2. A six-year study of the ecology and fisheries of the reef led to a set of management recommendations including a suggested marine reserve/park area (McManus and others 1992a, McManus and others 1992b, McManus and others 1995).

The need for the reserve was established by showing quantitatively that certain key species were over-fished, including a shell used in shell craft, *Strombus luanus* (Alino and Licuanan, *unpub.*), a sea urchin, *Tripneustes gratilla* (Trinidad and Pasamonte 1988, see also Junio-Menez and others 1995, Talaue-McManus and Kesner, 1995) and a rabbitfish, *Siganus fuscescens* (del Norte and Pauly 1990, McManus and others 1992a). Theoretical work indicated that the fishery as a whole was probably over-fished by more than twice the number of fishers required for optimal system output efficiency (McManus 1992). It was also clear that the habitat was rapidly degrading because of blastfishing, fishing with the use of sodium cyanide (for both aquarium fish and food fish), anchor damage, and possibly organic pollution leading to dominance in some areas by macroalgae rather than living coral.

Planning

The process of siting the reserve involved eight criteria:

1. Studies of the distributions in time and space of reef flat invertebrate species (de Guzman 1990), reef flat fish (Nanola 1995), reef slope fish (Nanola and others 1990), sea grasses (Fortes *unpub.*) and macroalgae (Trono and Ledesma 1990) indicated areas wherein most major subcommunities would be included, thereby optimizing location with regard to species diversity.

2. Studies of the distribution of fishing effort by gear and target species indicated areas which would include part, but not the majority, of each major fishery (McManus and others 1992a).

3. Observations and information from fishers were used to identify migratory routes of sea turtles and major fish species, including fish that migrated biannually and daily, particularly between seagrass and coralline areas or between the reef flat and open sea, so that portions of these routes could be protected (Aragones 1987, del Norte and others 1989, McManus and others 1992a).

4. Satellite image analysis and aerial surveys (by ultralight aircraft) were used to identify areas of dense concentrations of small channels cutting through the reef crest (McManus and others 1992a), to be protected based on the knowledge that reef fish often breed in such areas (see Thresher 1984).

5. Studies of the current structure (Villanoy, *unpub.*) indicated areas from which larvae and juveniles for a variety of species with short pelagic lives would be distributed to adjacent reef areas.

6. Studies of recoverable former mangrove stands identified areas suitable for the shoreward edge of a reserve (McManus and others 1992a).

7. Studies of the distributions of villages and individual houses indicated areas where the reserve could be located which would have the least effect with regard to excluding fishers from fishing grounds near to home (McManus and others 1992a).

8. Surveys of coral communities identified a single area of high aesthetic value to serve as a park to generate support funds from diving tourists (McManus 1992a).

On the basis of these criteria and others, a final reserve site was selected. The triangular reserve of approximately 6 km^2 would include a central park area of approximately 1 km^2 with permanent mooring buoys. Anchoring and fishing would be prohibited throughout the reserve system. Enforcement would be facilitated by the constant presence of ranger teams (working in shift rotations) headquartered in a stilt house on the reef flat near the reserve center. This site has housed in the past a stilt platform used by fish buyers, and is thus known to be suitable for long-term construction. The rangers would charge tourists to tie up to the buoys for diving, with funds contributing toward making the reserve self-sustaining (McManus and others 1992a).

Financing and Administration

The Philippine National Economic Development Authority indicated as early as 1993 that funds would be available to set up the reserve. It would have been reasonably simple for the government to have designated the area as either a national park, under the Department of Environment and Natural Resources, or a nationally sanctioned municipal fishery reserve under the Department of Agriculture. However, experience throughout the Philippines has indicated that small-scale coastal management policies originating with the national government have generally been either ineffective or counterproductive. Such an imposition of regulations from outside the community was unlikely to have maintained the local support and cooperation that the project would need to be successful. Basically, it was clear that the objective was not simply to make violations of reserve rules illegal, but rather to make them socially unacceptable (McManus 1988, McManus and others 1988, McManus and others 1992a).

The most effective way to create a reserve was to include the concept within a general project promoting municipal-level integrated coastal area development. Such a project was implemented in 1993. The project involves principally researchers from the University of the Philippines and the Haribon Foundation in a joint effort to promote community development in the area. The project is expected to last for five years, near the end of which the reserve concept would be introduced as a step toward ensuring the sustainable and optimal use of the reef.

As with most recent efforts of this kind, the current project relies heavily on the principal of empowerment–in this case, the enhancement of the villager's rights to manage their own resources, including the reef. Empowerment often involves a redistribution of power within the community, such that previous officials are replaced by others, often from a lower economic stratum. However, in times of need the fishers often have to borrow money for emergency food, medicine, or even repairs to the house, boat or gear. In the absence of small-scale loan institutions, the source of loans is generally the families of those who formerly held power. This tends to erode the empowerment efforts, and can lead to the deterioration of the entire development effort, including marine reserves. Thus, an emphasis is being placed on encouraging fishers to invest not only in children (a common form of retirement security), but in bank accounts as well. A small-scale loan institution, similar to the Grameen Bank in Bangladesh (Serageldin 1995) would be particularly helpful in making villager empowerment sustainable, but no such institution is currently available in the area.

Conflicts with Non-IQL Planning

Unfortunately, the Bolinao reef system now faces a new threat. The area has been designated a site for the development of heavy industry. An open pit mine for limestone is expected to provide material for a large cement plant. The current plans for the mine, which could cover at least 2 km^2, site it up-current from the reef. Scientists believe that during typhoons, the sediments deposited during the operation will be washed onto the reef, killing the remaining corals. The operation would provide about 200 jobs. Of these, at least 100 would require college degrees, and be filled principally by outsiders. Thus, it appears that the livelihoods of 20,000 people could be jeopardized for the sake of 100 jobs which will last for less than a decade of mine operation. Other plans include the construction of a petrochemical plant on the porous limestone coast facing the reef. In the face of these threats, the survival of the reserve proposal is highly uncertain.

A Spratly Island Marine Park

Much of the coastal zone in the vicinity of the South China Sea is over-fished (McManus 1988). Much of this over-fishing is related to and compounded by problems associated with rapid human population growth. The intense competition for resources leads to the use of fishing gear which is formerly not socially acceptable, illegal, environmentally destructive and harmful to the user— a condition known as Malthusian over-fishing (Pauly and others 1989, Pauly 1990, McManus and others 1992a, McManus and others 1995, McManus *in press*). Thus, not only are the stocks of these highly diverse waters over-fished, but the environments which support the harvested species are being rapidly degraded because of blastfishing, cyanide fishing and other problems.

During the long-term study of the Bolinao reef complex, it was noted that adult fish were rare enough to make them unlikely sources of the relatively abundant juveniles inundating the reef slope every year. The level of fishing versus population density and other information confirmed that this situation was likely to be universal throughout the nations bordering the central South China Sea, with the exception of Brunei and some parts of Malaysia. A reanalysis of data published by Brothers and Thresher (1985) indicated that most reef fish lead pelagic lives ranging from a few weeks to two months before settling on a reef (McManus 1994). A review of current charts indicated that a dense area of reefs in the south-central South China Sea could be responsible, at different parts of the reversing monsoon cycle, for supplying impoverished reefs in the region with juvenile fish. This area, known as the Spratly Islands, was known to be subject to sporadic, often very destructive fishing in shallow reefs areas, but was subject to much less fishing pressure in general than the bordering, crowded coastlines (McManus 1993, McManus 1994).

Designated the "dangerous grounds" on navigation charts because of inadequate charting, the islands and reefs of the area are subject to overlapping claims by the Philippines, Taiwan and mainland China, Vietnam, Malaysia and Brunei. The conflict is commonly cited to be the major threat to regional security. A Naval clash in 1988 led to the sinking of a Vietnamese naval vessel and 78 lives lost. A history of arrests of one nation's fishers by another was followed recently by an international controversy on the construction by the Chinese of housing facilities on a structure known as Mischief Reef. Most claimants maintain troops on the reefs and islands, and some analysts believe that China's recent interest in obtaining aircraft carriers and submarines stems from a desire to dominate the archipelago. The strategic interest stems from the fact that an average of 300 ships pass by it each day and the area is believed to hold vast reserves of oil. A study of geological reports indicate that the probability of finding oil is actually much higher in surrounding shelf areas than in the Spratlys (McManus 1994). It is believed that the emphasis on oil is a tactic used by various countries to build up support for exploratory drilling, which would count favorably toward the sponsoring country in any future attempts to establish sovereignty under international law.

Planning

The publication of the concept for the park (McManus 1993, 1994) and several presentations by the author and others have generated considerable interest among regional marine scientists, many of whom have been involved in informal workshops on the conflict in the last two years. There have been very few productive official workshops on the Spratly Islands, and this has given weight to the informal workshop findings. The claims of oil have tended to complicate the more official negotiations. The informal workshops have led to a general acceptance by the claimant countries of the need for joint research, particularly with regard to the benefits of maintaining the area as a park. Plans for such research are now underway, and a search is on for appropriate sources of funding. Various leaders, including President Ramos of the Philippines have included environmental protection as a target in future negotiations.

The major step toward a more rational management system for the Spratly Islands would be a freeze on claims. As with Antarctica, a freeze on claims would involve an agreement among all claimants that following a certain date, no actions by any party would be valid for the establishments of a claim in an international court. This would not only pave the way for positive collaborative actions, but would also diminish the need to exaggerate the desirability of the area as a site for oil exploration. Although there are many difficulties in getting signatures from both Taiwan and mainland China on a treaty, the two are involved in the Asian Development Bank (ADB). Professor Lotilla of the University of the Philippines has suggested that an agreement for a freeze on claims could possibly be part of a program of the ADB.

The size of the park would vary considerably depending on the reefs included and the manner in which boundaries were drawn. One could assume that it would cover between 200,000 and 300,000 km^2, making it second among marine parks only to the Great Barrier Reef Marine Park (344,000 km^2) in size. A park of this size would require aircraft and fast, ocean-going patrol boats for supervision. A headquarters could be established on one of the larger central islands, and one or more outposts established on islands where military facilities and air strips already exist.

There are a number of feasible options for park funding. Four of the six countries are eligible for aid as developing countries, and arrangements could be made involving debt-for-nature financing. Taiwan and Brunei would have less need for such assistance. Alternatively, or perhaps as a way of raising initial capital, developed countries which are highly dependent on the adjacent sea lane (for example, Japan, Russia, Canada and the U.S.) might be approached for funds directed at ensuring peaceful maintenance of the sea lane and its associated park.

Once established, a marine park could be administered by a contracted nongovernmental organization (NGO), perhaps supervised by a panel of representatives from the claimant countries. Because efficient management would involve the use of aircraft and watercraft, the NGO could also be tasked with search and rescue functions, buoy and channel maintenance, pollution prevention and anti-piracy actions. All of these functions are gravely needed in this area, particularly because of the heavy shipping traffic of the adjacent waters. The provision of a large, pirate-free boating area would boost regional yacht-building industries. Additionally, the fragile nature of the small island ecosystems would rationally lead to an avoidance of the construction of tourist facilities on the islands, and instead a reliance on live-aboard tourist boats. This would be a further boost to certain boat-building and tourism sectors.

Contrasting the Large and Small MPAs Relative to the IQL

Both the Bolinao and Spratly Island MPAs are focused on helping small-scale fishing communities in an intergenerational context. The Bolinao MPA is designed to ensure that the local reef system remains productive over a long time frame as a source of income and food for Bolinao residents. It would also benefit coastal communities located down-current (principally north) by providing recruits to stabilize harvestable stocks on other reefs, as well as the associated biota constituting their support systems. If indicators of success were obvious, such as the presence of marked increases in annual catches, the MPA would serve as a model for other small community reserves.

The Bolinao reserve and most potential emulations would directly benefit large numbers of poor fishing families. Predicting this benefit is not dependent on economic assumptions involving a trickle-down of the indirect effects of having produced greater wealth among sectors which were financially better off to begin with. The direct benefits to communities from a marine rescue should be contrasted with the alternative strategy of developing Bolinao as a center for cement and petrochemical handling. The latter strategy provides a few hundred jobs, in contrast to the thousands offered by the fishery and reef-associated tourism. Most of the income from the industrial approach would be concentrated in a few families, and benefits to the majority could only come indirectly. The cement mine is clearly a case of short-term exploitation which reduces options available to future generations.

The Spratly Island MPA is justified in part by the need to provide recruits of harvestable species (and supportive species) to fishing communities in an intergenerational, sustainable manner. The variability in ecological requirements of reef organisms makes it unlikely that small coastal reserves could sustain all important species without influxes of juveniles from larger reserves. These influxes are necessary not only to minimize and facilitate recuperation from local extinctions, but also to maintain genetic diversity within species and, with it, resistance to disease and deleterious environmental change.

However, the investment and planning strategies differ greatly in the Spratly Island MPA. The Spratly Island MPA is clearly a top-down park, of necessity being initiated and managed at levels far above those of coastal beneficiaries. The Bolinao MPA would not be effective without strong local involvement in design and administration, as well as provincial and national government support, technical assistance and perhaps legislation, and would thus be a balanced example of co-management (Pomeroy and Williams 1994).

The potential Bolinao MPA tourists are primarily backpack tourists, looking to save money and experience culture in their quest to visit coral reefs. This group is typical of the clientele targeted by many small-scale tourist enterprises in coastal villages. Although the levels of spending are low, the beneficiaries of the spending tend to be the villagers, rather than corporate representatives, thus leading to greater equity and more alternative livelihoods to reduce pressure on the environment from over-harvest. The tourist clientele of the Spratly Island MPA would generally have to afford live-aboard dive boats; their individual spending levels will be higher, particularly in port cities and transit areas such as airports. The recipients of this spending, however, will generally be corporations involved in high quality hotels or outlets for mass-produced tourist items. The Bolinao MPA would be managed as a very small-scale enterprise, whereas the Spratly Island management system would more closely resemble the management of the Great Barrier Reef Marine Park, involving administrative hierarchies, more expensive boats and access to aircraft. The capitalization of the Bolinao project would be governmental, but maintenance funds might be largely derived over time from the tourist users. The capitalization of the Spratly Island Park would probably require intergovernmental funding, and this support would likely require constant renewal, as it would be difficult to generate sufficient funds from tourist users without degrading the island ecosystems with hotels and other facilities.

These examples are indicative of the vast range of approaches which will be necessary in the future to develop and maintain a reasonable system of marine protected areas for the tropical world. The State of the Reefs report of the International Coral Reef Initiative (Jameson and others 1995) calls for the setting aside of 20 percent of all reefs as reserves of various sizes, and a system of strategically located large reserves to help maintain inter- and intra-specific diversity. The protected areas should constitute parts of wider coastal zone planning initiatives, aimed at ensuring quality of life of local peoples. In the face of a high variability in anthropogenic and ecological situations around the world, such a task will require a very broad outlook on planning and investment frameworks.

References

Aragones, N.V. 1987. *Taxonomy, Distribution, and Relative Abundance of Juvenile Siganids and Aspects of the Padas Fishery in Bolinao, Pangasinan.* Marine Science Institute, University of the Philippines, Quezon City, Philippines. M.S. thesis.

Brothers, E.B. and Thresher, R.E. 1985. "Pelagic Duration, Dispersal, and the Distribution of Indo-Pacific Coral Reef Fishes." In: M.L. Reaka (ed.) *The Ecology of Coral Reefs.* Symposia Series for Undersea Research, NOAA's Undersea Research Program, 3(1): 53-69.

de Guzman, A.B. 1990. *Community Structure of Macrobenthic Invertebrates on Exploited Reef Flats of Santiago Island, Bolinao, Pangasinan.* Marine Science Institute, University of the Philippines, Quezon City, Philippines. M.S. thesis.

del Norte, A.G.C. and D. Pauly. 1990. "Virtual Population Estimates of Monthly Recruitment and Biomass of Rabbitfish, *Siganus Fuscescens,* off Bolinao, Northern Philippines," 851 54. In R. Hirano and I. Hanyu (eds.) *The Second Asian Fisheries Forum.* Asian Fisheries Society, Manila, Philippines.

del Norte, A.G.C., C.L. Nanola, J.W. McManus, R.B. Reyes, W.L. Campos and J.B.P. Cabansag. 1989. "Over-Fishing on a Philippine Coral Reef: A Glimpse into the Future," 3087 97. In O.T. Magoon, H. Converse, D. Miller, L.T. Tobin and D. Clark (eds.) *Coastal Zone '89: Proceedings of the Sixth Symposium on Coastal and Ocean Management, 11-14 July 1989.* Charleston, S.C. vol. 4. American Society of Civil Engineers, New York, NY.

Fortes, M.D. 1995. *Seagrasses of East Asia: Environmental and Management Perspectives.* RCU/EAS Technical Report Series No. 6. UNEP.

Jameson, S., J.W. McManus, and M.D. Spalding. 1995. *State of the Reefs: Regional and Global Perspectives.* An International Coral Reef Initiative Executive Secretariat Background Paper. National Oceanic and Atmospheric and Administration, Silver Spring, MD.

Juino-Menez, M.A., N.N.D. Macawaris, and H.G.P. Bangi. 1995. "Potentials of Sea Urchin Culture as a Resource Management Strategy." 219-27 In: M.A. Juinio-Menez and G.F. Newkirk (eds.) *Philippine Coastal Resources under Stress. Selected Papers from the Fourth Annual Common Property Conference held in Manila, Philippines, June 16-19, 1993.* Coastal Resources Research Network, Biology Dept., Dalhousie University, Halifax, Nova Scotia and Marine Science Institute, University of the Philippines, Diliman, Quezon City, Philippines. 240 p.

McManus, J.W. 1992. "How Much Harvest Should There Be?" 52-56. In J.W. McManus, C. Nanola, C.R. Reyes, and K. Kesner. *Resource Ecology of the Bolinao Coral Reef System.* ICLARM Studies and Reviews 22. 117 p.

McManus, J.W. 1993. "The Spratly Islands: A Marine Park Alternative." *Naga: The ICLARM Quarterly.* 15(3):4-8.

McManus, J.W. 1994. "The Spratly Islands: A Marine Park?" *Ambio* 23(3): 181-86.

McManus, J.W., Nanola, C., Reyes, R., and Kesner, K. 1993. "The Bolinao Coral Reef Resource System." 193-211. In: M.A. Juinio-Menez and G.F. Newkirk (eds.) *Philippine Coastal Resources under Stress. Selected Papers from the Fourth Annual Common Property Conference held in Manila, Philippines, June 16-19, 1993.* Coastal Resources Research Network, Biology Dept., Dalhousie University, Halifax, Nova Scotia and Marine Science Institute, University of the Philippines, Diliman, Quezon City, Philippines.

McManus, J.W. 1988. "Coral Reefs of the ASEAN Region: Status and Management." *Ambio* 17(3): 189-93.

McManus, J.W., E.M. Ferrer and W.L. Campos. 1988. "A Village-Level Approach to Coastal Adaptive Management and Resource Assessment (CAMRA)," 381-86. In J.H. Choat, D. Barnes, M.A. Borowitzka, J.A. Coll, P.J. Davies, P. Flood, B.G. Hatcher, D. Hopley, P.A. Hutchings, D. Kinsey, G.R. Orme, M. Pichon, P.F. Sale, P. Sammarco, C.C. Wallace, C. Wilkinson, E. Wolanski and O. Bellwood (eds.)

Proceedings of the Sixth International Coral Reef Symposium, 8-12 August 1988. Townsville, Australia. vol. 2. Sixth International Coral Reef Symposium Executive Committee, Townsville, Australia.

McManus, J.W., Nanola, C., Reyes, R., and Kesner, K. 1992a. "Resource Ecology of the Bolinao Coral Reef System." *ICLARM Studies and Reviews* 22.

McManus, J.W., Nanola, C., Reyes, R., and Kesner, K. 1992b. "Resource Ecology of the Bolinao Coral Reef System." *Naga: The ICLARM Quarterly* 15(3): 43-45.

McManus, J.W. *In Press*. "Social and Economic Aspects of Reef Fisheries and Their Management." In: N. Polunin and C. Roberts (eds). *Coral Reef Fisheries*. Chapman and Hall.

Nanola, C.L. Jr., J.W. McManus, W.L. Campos, A.G.C. del Norte, R.B. Reyes Jr., J.P.B. Cabansag and J.N.D. Pasamonte. 1990. "Spatio-Temporal Variations in Community Structure in a Heavily Fished Forereef Slope in Bolinao, Philippines," 377-80. In R. Hirano and I. Hanyu (eds.) *The Second Asian Fisheries Forum*. Asian Fisheries Society, Manila, Philippines.

Nanola, C.L. Jr. 1995. "Distribution Patterns of Nocturnal Seagrass Fishes on the Reef Flat of Santiago Island, Bolinao, Philippines." Marine Science Institute, University of the Philippines, Quezon City, Philippines. M.S. thesis.

Pauly, D. 1990. "On Malthusian Over-Fishing." *Naga: The ICLARM Quarterly*, 13(1): 3-4.

Pauly, D., G. Silvestre and I.R. Smith. 1989. "On Development, Fisheries and Dynamite: A Brief Review of Tropical Fisheries Management." *Natural Resources Modeling* 3(3): 307-29.

Pomeroy, R.S. and M.J. Williams. 1994. *Fisheries Co-Management and Small-Scale Fisheries: A Policy Brief*. International Center for Living Aquatic Resources Management, Manila.

Serageldin, I. 1995. *Nurturing Development: Aid and Cooperation in Today's Changing World*. World Bank, Washington, D.C.

Talaue-McManus, L. and K.P.N. Kesner. 1995. "Valuation of a Philippine Municipal Sea Urchin Fishery and Implications of Its Collapse." 229-39. In: M.A. Juinio-Menez and G.F. Newkirk (eds.) *Philippine Coastal Resources under Stress. Selected Papers from the Fourth Annual Common Property Conference held in Manila, Philippines, June 16-19, 1993*. Coastal Resources Research Network, Biology Dept., Dalhousie University, Halifax, Nova Scotia and Marine Science Institute, University of the Philippines, Diliman, Quezon City, Philippines.

Thresher, R.E. 1984. *Reproduction in Reef Fishes*. TFH Publications, Inc. Neptune City, New Jersey, U.S.A.

Trinidad-Roa, M. and J.N. Pasamonte, 1988. *Population and Culture Studies of Sea Urchins in Bolinao, Pangasinan*. Annual Project Report. Marine Science Institute, University of the Philippines, Diliman, Quezon City, Philippines.

Trono, G.C. Jr. and A.O. Luisma. 1990. "Seasonality of Standing Crop of a Sargassum (Fucales, Phaeophyta) Bed in Bolinao, Pangasinan, Philippines." *Hydrobiologia* 204/205: 331-38.

Sustainable Financing of Protected Areas in Southern Sinai

Michael Pearson, Protectorates Department
Egyptian Environmental Affairs Agency

Abstract

The Egyptian Environmental Affairs Agency (EEAA), having executive authority over Protected Areas in the Arab Republic of Egypt, has established a principle of non-formal partnerships with private sector investors in development areas adjacent to its Protected Areas in Southern Sinai. These partnerships have now formed the basis for unique levels of cooperation between investors, hotel managers and the Agency represented by its Protectorates staff in South Sinai. This cooperation has permitted the EEAA to approve the implementation of an "Environmental Cost Recovery Charge" to sustainably finance its Protectorates program in South Sinai.

The Government of the Arab Republic of Egypt (GOE), recognizing the importance of South Sinai's natural resources to both national and regional economic development objectives, is currently committed to a program which will protect 12,500 km^2 of coastal and desert ecosystems in the South Sinai Governorate. This program, implemented with technical assistance from the European Union, has established management and conservation measures for 52 percent of the Egyptian littoral on the Gulf of Aqaba, including the Ras Mohammed National Park, Managed Resource Protected Areas at Nabq and Abu Galum and the Saint Katherine Protected Area. These protected areas will now be expanded to include the Taba Natural Monument and, following a request from the Ministry of Tourism, the remaining Egyptian littoral on the Gulf of Aqaba.

The program has been financed by the GOE (48 percent) with support from the European Union (52 percent). Additional finance has been secured through the collection of entrance fees–1,160,000 LE-1994, but these revenues will not achieve program sustainability. To overcome this deficiency, the EEAA has approved the application of an Environmental Cost Recovery Charge (ECRC) that will ensure that sufficient funds are generated to meet all program requirements. The application of this charge has been elaborated in close cooperation with private sector interests in South Sinai. The Private Sector recognizes the direct economic benefits derived from the Protectorates program and actively participates in its implementation. The program will be self-sustaining by the end of 1996. Furthermore, it will become a net contributor to the EEAA Environmental Fund, will contribute to the funding of selected environment projects proposed by the South Sinai Governorate, and will not require support from Central Government Funds.

Development of a Tourism-Based Economy in South Sinai: The Role of Protected Areas

South Sinai's proximity to European tourism markets and the Egyptian requirement for foreign exchange generated from tourism have, together, resulted in the rapid expansion of tourism facilities and associated infrastructure. Expansion of a tourism based local economy is reflected in the number of beds available in Sharm el Sheikh; 1,030 in 1988 and an expected 12,248 by the end of 1995 (completed hotels and hotels due to open by the end of 1995). A development ceiling for resort facilities in Sharm el Sheikh has been set at 23,000 beds. Conservative estimates based on an average annual occupancy of 70 percent (National Park surveys) suggest that 520,000 visitors will access the Sharm el Sheikh development area in 1995.

The environmental consequences of tourism activities on coral reef ecosystems are well documented. in Egypt, tourism developments constructed on the Red Sea coast at Hurghada are a case in point. Poor planning and unregulated development have modified coastlines through infilling of back reef areas. Coral reefs and all associated marine ecosystems have been severely damaged by siltation, anchor damage, abrasion collection and waste water discharges.

In South Sinai, regardless of the rate of development, regulatory measures established by the EEAA, have effectively limited direct and indirect damage to coral reefs and associated ecosystems. Staff of the National Park have adopted a non-confrontational approach to resource management to achieve conservation objectives in development areas fronting protected coastlines. Regulatory measures are implemented by EEAA (Protectorates) staff in Southern Sinai who liaise on a regular basis with investors through:

- The assessment and evaluation of development concepts to identify elements that may be inconsistent with Protectorate regulations or may violate setback regulations.

- The provision of free consultancy services throughout the construction phases to evaluate project infrastructure, propose beach solutions and determine access requirements to limit damage to fringing coral reefs.

- Continuous inspection of construction sites to ensure that developers adhere to all regulations.

- Personalized service, on demand.

- The provision of extension services to hotel management and staff.

- Training of hotel staff to enforce Protectorate regulations on reefs fronting their property. In particular, to control access over back reef areas, prevent feeding of reef fish, and prevent the collection of marine fauna, shells or fossil corals. These staff are issued uniforms identical to those worn by EEAA staff.

- Installation and maintenance of moorings at all designated dive sites (anchoring is forbidden).

- Authorization to use the official National Parks logo for advertising and marketing (on request).

Investors, hotel management and dive center operators recognize that the existence of the National Park and the Protectorates network in Southern Sinai has been instrumental in their own success. As such, property values have increased, prices for tour packages have remained consistently higher than those offered in Hurghada, demand for the area is increasing and media coverage has increased following recognition that rapid tourism development is being realized without undue damage to those resources that have engendered it (coral reefs, water quality, beaches, coastlines).

The continued existence of the National Park and Protectorates network in Southern Sinai is now an essential component of the national economic development strategy for the Egyptian Gulf of Aqaba region. As such, and following a request from investors in the northern Gulf, the Ministry of Tourism requested that all coastlines on the Gulf of Aqaba be provided with the same measure of protection and service afforded to investors in Sharm el Sheikh. This extension has been approved by all parties and will be formalized following signature of a Prime Ministerial Decree to that end.

Continued expansion of the Protectorates network in Southern Sinai will obviously increase operating and development costs. Recognizing that the current entrance fee structure will not be sufficient to achieve sustainability, EEAA staff in South Sinai have been working closely with investors and managers, to design a revenue generating scheme that will guarantee sufficient funding for all Protectorate programs and operations.

The "Environmental Cost Recovery Charge"

The basic premise behind the cost recovery charge is that all investors, managers and dive center operators benefit from the existence of the National Park and Protectorates Network in South Sinai. Likewise, all visitors to the area benefit from their natural resources and from management policies aimed at maintaining those resources in sound condition.

At present, only those visitors accessing the National Park at Ras Mohammed are being charged an entrance fee. These visitors represent 18 percent of those individuals using resources contained within the declared boundaries of the National Park (Park + adjacent protected coastal areas). Given that all coastlines fronting tourism development areas are protected and managed by the EEAA, then all individuals accessing any coral reef or beach area are benefiting from the protection of those resources. As such, all visitors and residents should be charged a nominal fee to use and enjoy protected resources.

The above argument was presented to private sector interests in the area prior to formal discussion with the EEAA. In all cases the concept was supported. Means of implementation were then formulated jointly with hotel managers. The concept was then presented to the EEAA and the Minister responsible for Environmental Affairs. In both cases the concept was approved in principle and will be applied as of 1 January 1996.

Implementing the "Environmental Cost Recovery Charge"

Discussions with private sector interests in the area have suggested that the Environmental Cost Recovery Charge will be levied by each hotel for each individual overnight stay. To introduce the program, and for a one year period (1996), the charge will be set at L.E. 0.5/US$ for Egyptians and non-Egyptians. The charge will then be increased in 1997 to L.E. 1.0/US$. This charge permitting access to all Protectorates in South Sinai collects fees from individuals not visiting a Protectorate but using resources contained in managed (Protected) coastlines. Residents and their families will be charged an annual fee of L.E. 150. Home owners renting their properties will be charged an annual fee based on the number of months their property is rented. This fee will be included in the rental charges applicable to each property. Revenue of L.E. 5,725,280 (or US$1,688,873) is expected following the introduction of the charge at the L.E. 0.5/US$ rate (Table 1).

Hotel guests will be provided with brochures on arrival and cards as proof of payment. Residents will be provided with photographic membership cards valid for one year. Renters will use a similar card provided by Park Authorities, on request by the owner, and valid for the rental period. Bedouin residents will not be charged.

The EEAA will receive payments from hotels on a monthly basis. These will be paid into an audited EEAA account in Sharm el Sheikh. Random payment verifications will be carried out on the basis of guest registrations collected daily from each property by the Tourism Police. Payments received in Sharm el Sheikh will then be transferred to the EEAA in Cairo and deposited in the Agency's Environment Fund.

Table 1. Gulf of Aqaba Protectorates

Item	1994 Entrance Fees LE	1996 ECRC[†] LE
Income	1,160,000	5,725,280
Total Operating Costs	1,657,369	2,976,111
Disbursements (governorate, staff)	—	2,003,848
Balance	(497,369)	745,321

† ECRC: Environmental Cost Recovery Charge, to be applied as of 1 January 1996.

Recovery of Revenue to Ensure Sustainable Finance of Conservation Programs

Preliminary discussions with the EEAA and the Minister responsible for Environmental Affairs have led to the elaboration of procedures to recover revenue on deposit in the Environment Fund.

The proposed procedure would establish a board of trustees representing private sector interests in the area and members of the EEAA. The board would receive an annual audited statement of accounts from the Protectorates Department and would review budget proposals for the following financial year. The board would also approve the funds allocated to the South Sinai Governorate and the projects these would support. The decision of the board would be forwarded to the EEAA for approval by the Chief Executive Officer and the committee charged with disbursements from the Environment Fund.

The board of trustees would not have any authority over Protectorate operations but could comment on planned development activities or planned expenditures.

The establishment of the board would further cement the informal partnership existing between private sector interests in South Sinai and the EEAA.

Concluding Remarks

Private sector interests in Southern Sinai have recognized the benefits of the Governments natural resource management and conservation programs. The EEAA, charged with implementing these policies, has established a unique level of cooperation with commercial operators in the area which has led to the approval of an Environmental Cost Recovery Charge that will generate sufficient funds to ensure sustainable financing and support for its Protectorates programs in South Sinai. This funding mechanism will establish a precedent in Egypt and one which can be considered internationally as an alternative to standard entrance fee based systems.

Reference

El Hawary, Emad. 1995. *Economic Assessment of Ras Mohammed National Park.* Egyptian Environmental Affairs Agency, National Biodiversity Unit, Natural Protectorates Department.

Community Groups and the Protected Areas Resource Conservation Project

Robert Kerr
Planning Institute of Jamaica, PARC Project

Started in 1989, the Protected Areas Resource Conservation (PARC) Project is a joint initiative between the Government of Jamaica, the U.S. Agency for International Development (USAID) and The Nature Conservancy. PARC's principal objective is the establishment of a system of protected areas in Jamaica. This system was pioneered by two pilot parks: the Blue and John Crow Mountains National Park and the Montego Bay Marine Park. Both parks have been officially opened for the past two and three years, respectively.

The success of establishing protected areas in Jamaica has foundations in two areas:

- Sound appreciation of the diversity of stakeholders involved in natural resources management (largely locals, who are the *de facto* managers) and their critical role in the successful financing and management of both marine and terrestrial protected areas

- Development of strategy, methods and organizational form to create partnerships which convert resource-use conflicts into motive forces for conservation and sustainable development initiatives.

For both pilot parks in Jamaica, the conservation values (biodiversity and developmental) provided platforms for building and expanding partnerships with long term commitments to conservation.

The Montego Bay Marine Park was established in the country's busiest tourist center. Montego Bay receives 500,000 visitors annually, earning nearly $1 billion in revenue. People initially did not understand the purpose of a national park. While it was easy to imagine a fountain, with water springing up and surrounded by flowers in the mountains, it was much more difficult to conceptualize how a protected area would be accomplished in the sea.

In fact, the Montego Bay Marine Park has been managed for some time. There were fishermen setting traps to catch fish–and they knew how many traps they wanted to set. There were people using nets–and they were deciding that those nets should take anything that they could catch. Spear fishermen and dive operators–people anchoring boats on the reef–chose this as their approach to management. There are several rivers leading out into Montego Bay and decisions were made to use the rivers as a quick way of getting rid of garbage.

And a water commission has been pumping several million gallons a day of untreated sewage into the Bay because it was cheaper than maintaining a proper sewage system. This has all been a form of management–just not a sustainable one.

The real task of the PARC project has been to get people to see the resource differently. A new vehicle was needed, one which took the form of local advisory committees (LAC). In Montego Bay, a committee and round table was formed, where all people who use the resource and are dependent upon it could meet and talk. The LAC met monthly with involvement from private, public and government agencies. Community participation has been critical for creating the resource base for the long-term operations of the park (that is, financing through cash, in-kind donations and user fees).

The Re-Definition of Community

New partnerships and organizational relationships were identified as prerequisites for sustained protection of coastal resources. Bearing in mind that coastal resources provide diverse-use values from serving as waste disposal sinks, to being a source of staple diet, the stakeholders vary significantly in their level of dependency and geographical relationship to the coast. The factory or farm located twenty miles upstream of a river (which is used for their waste disposal and which may lead to a marine protected area), and the local trap fishermen, are both stakeholders with potentially conflicting resource use. This picture can even be complicated further if they belong to social groups which traditionally have had antagonisms based on privileges and oppressive social relationships. Methods of conflict resolution have become critical tools in addressing such situations.

Drawing on the experience of developing the Montego Bay Marine Park, community involvement in park design, establishment and monitoring represented a central theme. Because Montego Bay is the 'tourist capital' of Jamaica, user impact was a major management issue. Early in the process, spear fishermen were viewed by many stakeholders as a major problem in resource over-exploitation. Through a partnership effort, a program was established to train spear fishermen as snorkel guides for hoteliers and other private enterprises. Several private sector groups, even before training was completed, gave commitments to employ the trainees. This is a classic example of how partnerships and cooperation becomes an essential part of the process in resource management.

As a result of the fishing ban within the park, the subsequent increase in frequency and size of fish observed has been worth a thousand words in convincing stakeholders that zoning and others forms of restrictions are worthwhile. For community groups to maintain active stakeholder interest, management of resources should begin to show tangible results, within planned schedules. The results, whether positive or negative, need to be shared with the stakeholders as partners in resource management. The important role that information sharing plays in winning new partners and convincing them of the need for their practical support cannot be understated.

Jamaica has worked hard for independence and has worked hard to educate its people. Today Jamaica has a new citizen–one that is more aware and more capable, and wants to participate in decisions surrounding resource use and management. A serious problem facing Jamaica is a lack of a national policy on sustainable development which harmonizes the various sectors. For example, the tourism industry invites foreign visitors to come and swim, but the water commission may allow sewage to enter water nearby. A paradigm shift is needed in the way all resource management agencies view Jamaica's resources. Without such a policy, we will continue to try to create islands of sustainability within a sea of destruction.

In the past, there seems to have been a fear of partnerships. However, today NGOs are much more capable and willing to play a role in the management of the affairs that impact on their communities. The question of the most efficient organization channels for handling funds for protected areas management is an important financial consideration for donors and managers. Trust funds as a mechanism for receiving and managing funds and the delegation of operational responsibilities by governments to local NGOs or community co-management are all new possibilities. The best solution is to build teamwork through community groups, which include the various agencies, the private sector, and international funding agencies, to try and make the challenge of sustainable development one in which we can face.

Outline for Proposed Biodiversity Enterprise Fund for Latin America

Michael Rubino
International Finance Corporation

Objective: A private equity or venture capital fund (the Fund) is proposed to invest in and catalyze private investment in commercially viable sustainable uses of biological diversity.

Background: Biodiversity is threatened by some forms of development and protected or used sustainably by others. Forests and other natural habitats are under threat from increased population, pollution, and expansion of cropland and urban settlement. Although natural habitats are undervalued in commercial markets, the products represented by biological diversity have many ecological, human health, and food production values. In response to the threat, a variety of activities have been undertaken to protect and sustainably use biological resources. These actions culminated in the signing of the Convention on Biological Diversity (CBD) by 157 countries at the United Nations Conference on Environment and Development (UNCED) in Rio de Janeiro in June 1992. The Convention requires signatory countries to protect species by protecting natural habitats. The problems recognized by the Convention will not be solved unless the private sector contributes its vast technical, managerial, and financial resources and expertise.

The Market Opportunity: Conservation activities, government policies, and market demands for certified sustainable products are expanding markets for businesses in the following sectors: alternative agriculture (organic farming, aquaculture, and use of underutilized species), sustainable forestry, non-timber products from forests (NTFP) and wildlands (such as nuts, fruits, and palm oils), eco-tourism, biodiversity prospecting (for example, pharmaceuticals from plants), and pollution control and other activities that restore or take development pressure off of biodiversity resources. An assessment of the deal flow indicates that numerous projects exist in the agriculture and forestry sectors, several in NTFPs and eco-tourism, and only a handful in biodiversity prospecting.

Rationale for the Fund: There is an opportunity for a private equity fund to be a catalyst, to mobilize capital to invest in projects with other investors for the following reasons:

There are biodiversity business opportunities with the potential for both attractive rates of return on investment and biodiversity benefits.

Latin American and foreign investors perceive opportunities and have begun to invest in biodiversity projects in the $250,000 to $10 million project size range. These ventures are seeking capital but investment funds available to finance these projects are inadequate (local bank debt is at prohibitively high rates, the projects are too small for standard IFC and other institutional financing, bilateral agencies and foundations focus on NGO conservation activities and microenterprises, and project development costs are high).

Private sector investors (strategic, social investment funds, corporate) *and foundations are interested in investing in a fund* and in providing partnerships (for marketing, value added, technical resources, exit, and expansion). The Fund would allow institutions like IFC to invest in many small- and medium-sized enterprises through one investment in a financial intermediary (the Fund).

Governments are interested in providing grant funds to such a fund for project development costs, for screening biodiversity impacts, and to encourage the private sector to select/invest in projects with biodiversity benefits.

The proposed Fund would play a leading role in bringing together the investors, grant funds, and expertise and making these resources available to entrepreneurs.

Investment Focus: The Fund will focus its investments in alternative agriculture, sustainable forest management, eco-tourism, and non-timber products from forests and wildlands. Exceptional projects may also be considered in biodiversity prospecting, remediation activities that restore biodiversity, and activities in buffer areas around national parks. The Fund will largely make equity, equity-type, or convertible debt investments in such ventures. Projects must adhere to the World Bank Group's environmental guidelines such as the Bank's forest policy.

Potential Sponsors/Investors: Potential investors in the Fund include an American social investment fund, a private European venture fund in Latin America, three major U.S. foundations, Latin American businesses, and IFC. These strategic investors are well connected to potential fund managers and other investors (institutional investors, pension funds, individuals, companies).

Capital: $20-30 million fund. Capital committed could be increased after three years, if the Fund is investing in attractive deals.

Geographic Focus: Latin America.

Management: The manager will be an experienced fund manager with emerging market and biodiversity experience and willing to make a significant commitment to the effort. The manager will have project identification capabilities and existing field offices.

Risk Mitigation: Methods will be sought to encourage the Fund to invest in some projects that might not otherwise attract investment because project development costs are too high or expected rates of return are too low (risks too high) for the private sector. To cover or mitigate these costs and risks, grants from bilateral government donors and the GEF may be provided to the Fund for (1) project development or "front end capital" costs (many biodiversity projects require initial development work to prepare them for financing); and (2) part of the Fund management/overhead costs (these costs may be higher than the usual two or three percent of capital invested because of high project identification and screening costs). Other risk mitigation methods will also be considered.

Boards of Directors and Advisors: The board of directors will consist of representatives from investors in the Fund. Advisors of recognized expertise will advise the Fund on the suitability of deals/projects from the perspective of biodiversity conservation.

Investment Criteria: The criteria will include potential for solid returns on investment, sustainable uses of biodiversity, local joint venture partners, and proven technology (some newer technology if strategic partners share in the technology risks).

Structure: The Fund structure and location are to be determined. Investors will earn all income and capital appreciation generated by the Fund net of management fees and carried interest by the Fund manager.

Risks: These include insufficient deal flow; higher than anticipated project development/identification costs; lack of biodiversity standards for some sectors leaving projects open to criticism that they are not protecting or sustainably using biodiversity; high expectations placed on the Fund by NGOs; the financial, project, and management risks of smaller projects with inadequate financial resources and innovative technologies; and economic, political, and country risks.

Project Examples

1. *Alternative and certified organic agriculture, preservation of crop varieties, and development of underused species or agricultural products*

    - Production and marketing of organically produced fruits, vegetables, coffee, and other produce, cottons, natural dyes, and other products

    - Crops grown on "marginal" lands such as salt tolerant halophytes

    - Dozens of underutilized agricultural plant and animals species such as the oca (an Andean tuber), amaranth (grain), palm oils, and legume cover crops

    - Integrated pest management, biopesticides

    - Culture of species that are endangered in the wild (takes pressure off wild stock), for example, conch, Amazonian fish, crocodiles, caymans, and sea turtles.

2. *Timber from sustainable forest management*

    Some veneer mills will not purchase and some countries ban imports of tropical hardwoods. They are seeking wood certified (by NGO certification services) as coming from sustainable forest management operations. Companies undertaking selective logging and plantations of tropical hardwoods, are candidate investments for the Fund.

3. *Non-timber products from forest sand wildlands*

    Several companies and landholders in Latin America are extracting nuts, fruits, rubber, and oils from forest lands.

4. *Biodiversity prospecting*

    Extracts from plants and animals are used by the pharmaceutical and cosmetic industries and in agriculture. Two Andean region companies have been formed to work with local institutes and indigenous groups to develop extracts based on ethno-botanical knowledge to pharmaceutical and other larger companies. Major drug companies and several venture capital startups are looking at dozens of potential plant-based drugs. Already, three anti-cancer drugs based on plants earn about $1 billion per year in revenues.

5.   *Eco-tourism*

Some lodges/hotels follow eco-tourism practices linking travel in relatively pristine areas to the low impact use and conservation of the areas' natural resources. One group has proposed a $20 million business to purchase or build and then operate a dozen or more eco-tourism lodges in Latin America, perhaps in association with a major tour operator.

6.   *Remediation and pollution control activities that enhance/restore biodiversity*

*   Uses of wetlands, constructed wetlands, and duckweed/ macroscopic algae to treat or restore wastewaters

*   Remediation of toxic soils to restore the biodiversity of the soil.

Creating a Planning and Investment Framework through Partnerships:
The Biodiversity Conservation Network

Hank Cauley, Biodiversity Conservation Network
Biodiversity Support Program

The Biodiversity Conservation Network (BCN) is part of the Biodiversity Support Program (BSP), which is implemented as a consortium of three NGOs: World Wildlife Fund, The Nature Conservancy, and World Resources Institute. BCN funding comes from the U.S. Asia Environmental Partnership, which is part of USAID.

The BCN was established to (1) support site-specific efforts to conserve biodiversity at a number of sites across the Asia/Pacific region, and (2) evaluate the effectiveness of enterprise-oriented approaches to community-based biodiversity conservation. To achieve these goals, BCN brings together organizations in Asia, the Pacific, and the United States in active partnerships with local and indigenous communities. The program provides grants for projects that encourage the development of enterprises that are dependent on sustained conservation of local biodiversity. BCN provides financing for the enterprises and provides funds for the biological, social, and economic monitoring of the projects' impacts.

The BCN has funded six projects to help protect marine biodiversity. As examples, two BCN-funded projects are discussed below.

The Solomon Islands

The Arnavon Islands in the Solomon's are at the center of an area rich in marine and terrestrial biodiversity. They lie in the Manning Straits of the Solomon Islands midway between the islands of Santa Isabel and Choiseul. Three village complexes–Kia, Posarae, and Waghena–are near enough to the uninhabited Arnavons to permit regular visits there by fishermen and turtle hunters to harvest the Islands' resources. These three villages have disparate histories and economies, but for the purposes of conservation planning they are grouped into a Greater Arnavon Resource Management Area (GARMA).

The GARMA extends from the eastern end of Choiseul Province to the western end of Isabel province, and includes the small islands and ocean between these two points. It encompasses an area of 4,700 km^2 in a quadrangle roughly 140 kilometers east to west and 35 kilometers north to south.

The Arnavon Islands within the GARMA are one of the most important rookeries in the western Pacific for the endangered hawksbill turtle, and home to one of the world's largest nesting populations of the species. The marine environment of the GARMA also supports commercially valuable species such as beche-de-mer, trochus, black and gold lip pearl oysters, green snail, and giant clams.

The threat to the region's biodiversity is the over-harvesting of these marine products by the three local communities. Two of these three communities have had historical resource claims on the Arnavon Islands. However, the third community, which was moved to the region by the British in the mid-1960s from Kirabati, has emerged as the primary users of the marine resource. In the past, due to the conflicting resource rights issues, the relationship between the three communities has been highly confrontational.

The key players implementing the project to promote conservation and economic development within the GARMA are the three communities, an NGO (The Nature Conservancy), the Solomon Islands' Ministry of Forests, Environment, and Conservation, and several small businesses. This partnership will assist in getting products developed in the project site by a new deep-water fishing venture to national and international markets.

To date the partnership has strengthened conservation and economic development in the region by:

- Establishing a management committee for the broad resource area with representatives from the communities, NGO, and the government

- Drafting a management plan for the area that:
    - Establishes a core conservation area of 31 km^2 area surrounding the Arnavon Islands where no marine product commercial harvesting will be permitted for three years
    - Establishes a larger buffer zone of 83 km^2 area around the core with strict guidelines on what can and cannot be harvested over the next three years
    - Forms a squad of conservation officers drawn from the three communities whose role is to monitor the enforcement of conservation area regulations
    - Establishes mechanisms for addressing conflicts that might arise in the conservation area.

A primary reason for closing off some areas to marine product harvesting for several years, and allowing limited harvesting in others, is to determine sustainable harvest rates.

A third parallel activity involves developing a fishing enterprise whose viability rests on the conservation of the region's biodiversity. Part of this activity includes the following:

- With BCN funding, the NGO brought in a consulting firm specializing in market analysis and identifying enterprise opportunities.

- The NGO established a marketing cooperative that provides the infrastructure for storing fish locally, transporting them to Honiara, and linking up with wholesale buyers.

Finally, the NGO is also helping the three communities build their commitment to conservation through education programs focused on marine resources and providing training for sustainable resource management and business skills.

Although this project is only in its early stages, it appears that the strength of the partnership formed, although not a guarantee for success, at least ensures the ability of the collaborating team to deal with the critical emerging resource management issues.

All BCN-funded projects must have monitoring systems in place to assess the impact of the projects from social, biological, and economic perspectives. In time, the BCN and its grantee partners hope to take the lessons learned from projects to other sites.

Marine Biodiversity Prospecting in Fiji

On the island of Viti Levu in the coastal village of Ucunivanua, a Fijian NGO, SPACHEE, has joined up with the international NGO, Rainforest Alliance, to work with the indigenous coastal community. Other collaborators include the University of the South Pacific and a major pharmaceutical company.

To help meet the economic needs of the coastal community and emphasize the importance of their biodiversity, an enterprise is being developed to investigate the pharmaceutical potential of extracts of Fijian marine resources. A critical aspect of this program is to develop an agreement for just compensation (both short- and long-term) to the host country and local community in recognition of the potential value of these resources. The compensation will not only have a monetary component but will also include training and technology transfer to enhance the sustainability of the enterprise.

The compensation will increase local incomes by about 25 percent in the short-term and there is the potential for royalties down the road.

Marine biological prospecting will involve the pharmaceutical company, which will perform a range of bioactivity tests on up to 300 marine samples collected annually, and will also assist the University of the South Pacific in developing assays for tropical diseases. Finally, the pharmaceutical company has its own foundation which will invest up to $25,000 in community development projects.

It is important to note that no samples will be taken until the prospecting agreement between the community and the collaborators has been signed. Such a prospecting agreement will be novel in the Pacific and would provide a basis for similar regional agreements.

In this case, the critical elements of the partnership have been:

- The NGOs' and the University's intent to protect the rights of the coastal community in the writing of the prospecting agreement (as an example, using BCN funds, the community will have its own legal counsel)

- The pharmaceutical company's willingness to move forward on the overall project at a pace determined by the local partners.

These unique partnerships in the Solomon Islands and Fiji offer several generic lessons:

With respect to *Planning:*

- The NGOs took a lead role in bringing all of the key players to the table and establishing a common vision for what could be achieved.

- The NGOs worked with the communities to clearly define the marine and terrestrial resource collection rights issues.

- The NGOs arranged to bring in technical assistance to strengthen the partnership approach.

- All of the players committed to using a management committee as a vehicle for drafting a partnership plan and resolving issues.

From an *Investment* standpoint:

- The NGOs and the communities took a hard look at the *viability* of a resource-dependent enterprise: potential markets, the competition, cost structures for getting product to market, and the *sustainability* of competitive business advantages.

- The communities had to assess the *skills* of those members who will be involved in the marine-based enterprise, and the NGOs made a commitment to develop and enhance skills as required.

- Perhaps the most important lesson is the *commitment* by all of the players to a partnership structure. This partnership will address issues such as, how the benefits will be distributed within the community, and how to resolve conflicts between partners.

In conclusion, the key elements of success for the examples cited are (1) viable partnerships, (2) attractive economic alternatives, and (3) anticipating the fluid nature of resource management issues and putting the mechanisms in place to address such dynamic situations.

Question: I did not hear you mention the fisheries department of the State of Fiji as being involved [in the bioprospecting agreement]. They are the people who give the license to legally export material and to collect. If the government is not involved, and only the NGOs and indigenous people, then you may have a problem.

Response. (Hank Cauley). The government is involved; their role is not clearly defined at this time, and that is one thing that has to be resolved before finalizing the prospecting agreement.

Comment: (John McManus). Dr. Newman mentioned required approval from the fisheries boards. This is doubly important because in order to determine what is sustainable, they [fisheries boards] would have to look into the population dynamics of these organisms, and there are very few invertebrates for which we know anything about their population dynamics.

Comment: (David Newman). For example, we [NCI] are permitted to take a metric ton of *Lissodendoryx* [a sponge] from New Zealand territorial waters. The U.S. government commissioned a $30,000 ecological survey of the sponge bed before we took one sample. That information was made available to every NGO and everybody within New Zealand who wished to look at it. I have a permit that specifically restricts sample custody and transfer only to NCI, and otherwise can not go out of New Zealand.

Question: The Ras Mohammed Park is often talked about as a classic example of a resource being loved to death. I understand that there are problems with diver behavior there, and wondered if this was a misconception, or reality, and whether there are plans to educate divers more thoroughly in that area? Also, would designating larger and larger marine protected areas be contrary to conserving biodiversity?

Response: (Michael Pearson). You are referring to some of the articles that have been written recently, and unfortunately those articles are using incorrect figures. A figure which is very often quoted is 800,000 divers per year. This is not correct. Next year we expect to receive 500,000 visitors, of which only 35 percent are divers. All the diving centers have been trained by the national park to provide diver briefings. We are now starting a system by which all tour operators, which include diving center operators, must pass an exam that is a standardized approach to diving operations. If all of their staff does not pass the exam, they don't work. We have found, working with a Ph.D. student from York University in the U.K., that if you carry out a correct diving briefing after the first dive–we take a one dive sacrifice–that you reduce the damage substantially–down to 10 percent of the original damage levels. We have also found that if you control access over the back reef areas (we work very closely with the hotels by designing access points and the number allowed), we take a 1.5 m sacrificial section–we reduce damage to 10 percent of the original level. We are finding that these measure are very successful. Ras Mohammed is a dive site which has been heavily used in the past, but it is less used now. We have set a dive site management program there by limiting the diving centers to five days out of seven, and only one boat per day. Given the nature of tourism development in the area, given the problems associated with the peace process, given the activities which are planned for the area, the government has asked that coastlines be regulated for specific developments (for example, the area north of Ras Mohammed up to the Gulf of Suez is being planned for light industry). The protected areas section of the Environment Agency is the only executive branch the government has. As such, the government relies on its protected areas network to effectively manage large sections of coastline. So, it's not that we're managing a small Ras Mohammed, or other area, we're establishing a principle of large-scale coastal zone management through an integrated approach which brings in investors, with the government together. We provide free consultancy services and do the job we have to do. This approach is not limited only to the coastal area–we have 9,000 km^2 in the middle of the Sinai which was declared to protect it against tourism, and we are setting standards and exams. So, it takes time, but in six years it's not too bad.

V. Group Discussion

Introduction

Marea Hatziolos, Environment Department
World Bank

In many ways this is the most important section of the workshop, because it allows us to discuss in greater detail many of the themes introduced earlier in the day. Before opening the floor to general discussions, we'll begin this session with a brief look at two different kinds of partnerships that are beginning to mobilize support for coral reef conservation at the international, national, and local levels–the International Coral Reef Initiative, and the Coral Reef Alliance.

It is apparent that partnerships will be crucial to the success of sustainable financing initiatives. Partnerships between government, the private sector, local community groups, NGOs, as well as the scientific community will be needed to provide support and ideas for improved use and management of coral reefs.

The International Coral Reef Initiative

Susan Drake
U.S. Department of State

Just a year ago, it was difficult to generate enthusiasm about a potential International Coral Reef Initiative (ICRI). However, the World Bank has been proactive in supporting efforts for marine conservation, including ICRI, and the presentation of the four-volume report *A Global Representative System of Marine Protected Areas* dovetails very well with the goals and objectives established for ICRI.

The Coral Reef Initiative was established approximately a year and a half ago, and began by organizing a group of scientists, NGOs and public officials together to determine the need in addressing the problems of coral reefs. The State Department's involvement was based on its interest in integrated coastal zone management, and using coral reefs as an important focal point that would elicit interest and public involvement in the process. Four principals were determined to make up the essence of the initiative:

1. Ownership through partnership
2. Integration
3. Coordination
4. Participation.

Ownership was developed by bringing together scientists, managers, diplomats, NGOs, trade and tourism groups, representatives from the World Bank, Asian Development bank and others. Thus, all the stakeholders were organized, with the exception of individuals at the very local level. The key to success is to ensure that all potential stakeholders have a sense of ownership of ICRI. Three central points of ICRI are sustainable management and use of coral reefs, research and monitoring, and capacity building.

Taking into consideration the four elements of ICRI, the concept of partnership was put forward. Although the term has evolved over the progress of ICRI, partnerships were initially donor driven. The countries of the U.S., U.K. France, Sweden, Japan, and Australia all contributed resources to bring the initiative together. However, the term partnership evolved to include an endorsement of a "Call to Action"–calling interested participants to become involved with each of the three central points. After this call to action, a "Framework for Action" was developed by all of the stakeholders at the ICRI initiating workshop, held in Dumagette City, Philippines in May, 1995, which provided an implementing document for the call to action. The Framework for Action endorses the report presented at the beginning of this workshop in priority designation of coral reef marine protected areas. Thus, partnership is now defined as stakeholder endorsement and commitment to the ICRI Call to Action, involvement in the Framework for Action at international, national, regional and local levels, and supporting development of the International Oceanographic Commission Global Coral Reef Monitoring Network. This network is intended to obtain and share data on coral reefs at the local level throughout the world.

ICRI is now focused on six regional workshops in the coming year (the wider Caribbean, the Red Sea, the Western Indian Ocean, the Pacific, East Asia, and South Asia). The intent is to involve regional, national and local communities to examine how the Framework for Action can be implemented in specific cases.

ICRI's goal is to see that National Coral Reef Initiatives are developed for countries worldwide, but that the content of these Initiatives are not dictated. Rather, they are products that are developed and "owned" by stakeholders at each national level.

A second focus of ICRI is to incorporate the principles and actions of the Framework into upcoming meetings, such as the Biodiversity meeting, meetings on land-based sources of marine pollution, and the Conference on Environmentally Sustainable Development.

The ICRI is not meant to be a new program. There are clearly enough existing marine programs that can be used and leveraged to develop creative financing strategies to implement the Framework for Action. As examples, the World Bank could give preference in assistance to those countries that have endorsed the Call to Action and Framework for Action. Also, expansion of the Bank's portfolio to include projects that involve coral reefs for sustainable use and management would further ICRI's purpose. Finally, the World Bank may be able to encourage public/private partnerships for lending opportunities to developing nations.

The CORAL Diver Network

Stephen Colwell
The Coral Reef Alliance

The Coral Reef Alliance (CORAL) represents one small partner in coral reef conservation–scuba divers and the diving community. CORAL acts as a catalyst for coral reef conservation by encouraging and assisting scuba divers and the diving industry to act as stewards of the reefs.

This summary addresses two issues:

- The CORAL Diver Network–how divers can act as an alternate source of funding for reef conservation

- The International Year of the Reef–1997, how it will contribute to coral reef conservation.

CORAL has recently completed the first stage of a survey of divers across North America. All statistics are only approximate, but they do give some valuable insight into the potential of divers to contribute to coral reef conservation.

The CORAL Diver Network

CORAL is creating a global network of divers concerned about the condition of coral reefs. Known as the CORAL Diver Network, and using the Internet, newsletters and meetings to communicate with each other, this group serves several important functions. The CORAL Diver Network is:

- An active, vocal constituency for coral reef conservation

- A channel for rapid distribution of information about coral reefs

- A source of volunteers and technical expertise to assist in conservation projects

- A source of funds to support coral reef conservation.

This summary focuses on using divers as a source of conservation funding.

CORAL is currently building a Coral Reef Conservation Fund that will serve as a permanent Trust to support coral reef conservation and research. CORAL's goal is to reach an endowment of $10 million, and use the proceeds to create small grants of $5,000 to $20,000 to support reef conservation projects, particularly in developing countries.

What is the potential of divers as a conservation funding source?

Scuba divers constitute a large, affluent demographic group in industrialized countries. There are over 6 million certified scuba divers in the industrialized countries, and each year over 600,000 new scuba divers are certified. Diving certification is growing at approximate 10 percent per year in the U.S., and two to three times that fast in other major markets such as Japan and Western Europe.

Demographic studies show that many of these divers match the profiles for good prospects for charitable giving. The majority of divers are college educated and have annual incomes exceeding $70,000, and a growing percentage of new divers are women.

Scuba divers also have a vested interest in keeping coral reefs alive. They spend over $1 billion annually to dive at coral reef destinations. International dive tourists take an average of 1.25 dive trips a year; stay an average of eight days per trip; and spend approximately $3,200.

Despite these promising statistics, there is little evidence that divers are currently contributing much to the financial support of coral reefs, except indirectly through the revenue earned by coral reef destinations.

There are a number of options for raising funds from divers for conservation.

- Taxes on Divers. Taxes on divers–such as hotel and tourist taxes–are already used in many places. Unfortunately, since the funds are rarely earmarked for reef conservation, the impact is probably negligible.

- User and Entrance Fees. Properly planned, designed and implemented, fees can be a useful source of funds, particularly if used in Marine Protected Areas where NGOs have been given the responsibility of managing the MPA, and the funds go directly to support conservation. There is a great deal of sensitivity to fees within the dive industry right now; the feeling is that divers are unfairly singled out. It is important to remember when we talk about public/private partnerships that partnerships are built, not created. The failure to build consensus support for user fees within the diving community–to show the need and guarantee that the funds will go directly to conservation–will torpedo well-intentioned efforts to implement a fee system.

- Direct Contributions to Coral Reef Conservation Programs. This is the traditional funding approach taken by NGOs. On-site donations can be profitable for some destinations, particularly through the sale of T-shirts and other items. On the other hand, donations to centralized organizations that can redistribute funds are crucial if we are to capture the large percentage of divers who do not dive frequently, and if we want to support areas with great need but a small number of dive visitors.

The prospects for raising funds appear to be good; several studies have come up with remarkably similar numbers. Two separate surveys of divers indicated that over 90 percent would be willing to pay fees to dive in MPAs. In the Bonaire study, 92 percent said they would be willing to pay $10 extra and 48 percent said $30.

In our most recent survey 89 percent of divers surveyed said they would be willing to make a financial contribution to an organization such as CORAL to support coral reef conservation.

These figures suggest that divers do have substantial potential as a source of conservation funds. Is it a sustainable funding mechanism? The answer is a cautious "yes," but will vary by destination, depending upon the current condition of the reefs, the number and size of competing users of the reefs, the management and conservation skills applied, the number of divers who visit coral reefs and many other factors. One thing is clear: Divers will only become a sustainable source of funding for coral reef conservation if they are: (1) educated about the threats to coral reefs; and (2) directly asked to help.

The International Year of the Reef–1997

The International Year of the Reef (IYOR) is a major effort to assess the condition of reefs worldwide, to document patterns of degradation and seek their causes, to educate users and the public on the values of reefs and to assist in the development of strategies to advance their recovery and promote their sustainable management. It will provide a global context for national and regional efforts and a handle for publicity and fund-raising activities, stimulating organizations and institutions with common interests and aims. It will be complementary to activities such as the International Coral Reef Initiative (ICRI) and other local, national, regional or international programs.

At the 1993 colloquium in Miami, Florida on the Global Status of Coral Reefs, a clear consensus emerged among scientists that many reefs are in decline worldwide, notably in areas adjacent to human population centers. It was also clear from a region-by-region review of what is known of the world's reefs that basic information on their condition is inadequate. 1997 was therefore declared as the Year of the Reef and has since been renamed the International Year of the Reef. The IYOR will be launched at the 8th International Coral Reef Symposium to be held in Panama, 24-29 June 1996.

IYOR will have a two-pronged approach, one through the scientific community, and one through the NGO community. The scientific community will be responsible for undertaking coral reef assessment, monitoring and other relevant research aimed at creating a more complete picture of the condition of the world's reefs, and a better understanding of how we can help them stay alive. The NGO community will take the lead in developing public awareness activities designed to highlight the value of coral reefs and the serious threats faced by coral reefs. Both approaches will complement each other: methods developed for reef assessment can be used by the NGO community to evaluate conservation programs; and publicity and education campaigns carried out by NGOs will lead to wider support for scientific work and to the release of funds necessary for research. Both approaches will contribute to the development of new and more effective strategies for sustainable coral reef conservation.

There is a great deal of preparatory work that needs to be done now in order to make IYOR–1997 a success. CORAL invites all readers to review their organization's programs and goals and see how each can make a contribution to IYOR.

Comment: (Marea Hatziolos). I think we need to look further at the notion of consumer surplus–that margin of additional cost that consumers are willing to pay for an exceptional experience–as a way to limit access to certain MPAs because their carrying capacity is being exceeded. One example is in the Philippines, on the island of Palauan, where a resort has been established with clientele in the higher income brackets. This resort is the result of a joint venture operation with the private sector (that is, the Japanese and Philippine private sector in cooperation with the Philippine government). The fees to use the resort are quite high, but a sizable portion goes directly into supporting the local community. This is a good example of an eco-tourism project that is generating benefits to local communities, enhanced fisheries for the local fisherman, as well as meeting its conservation objectives.

Question: At the CSD [Conference for Sustainable Development] and the COP [Conference of Parties], it appears as if the environmental movement globally is fire-fighting. There is a convention on almost every aspect of the ecosystem: desertification, ozone layer, forest–there seem to be endless conventions and it's hard to keep track of what is happening. It seems to me a lot of the problems stem from the absence of a new policy on natural resources. If we have been operating with the resources as if they are infinite, and clearly they are not, and if you look at the amount of money being pumped into traditional forms of using the resources versus what goes into conservation, then you'll in fact see that perhaps there is not really a change of policy and momentum. Is there anything that can be done to bring in various countries, (for example, the U.S. and others) and begin to put a partnership together between the private sector, governments and NGOs to redefine or rethink national policy or natural resource use?

Response: (Susan Drake). The question gets to a fundamental root of whether the mechanisms being used are currently in the international realm effective on environmental problems and degradation. With respect to coral reefs, what ICRI is trying to do is revolutionary–in that we have developed a partnership of NGOs, UN bodies, multilateral developmental banks, and governments. In fact, governments are limited in what they can do, and therefore, much of the partnership has to rely on NGOs with support from the banks and UN organizations. In essence, your question is "Should we not be thinking of a completely new approach to environmental issues?" and I think yes, we should. In the case of many of these conventions, I think the reason why the Coral Reef Initiative to this point (granted, it has just been launched) has been successful, is because it has not been under the UN. Based on past experiences, given the level of politicalization and consensus-based modes that can occur within the UN, oftentimes new and progressive ideas are prohibited from moving forward within reasonable time frames necessary. ICRI is trying to utilize existing mechanisms to the benefit of the partnership that has been created. For example, in the case of the Conference of Parties and the Land-Based Sources of Pollution, we are hoping we can integrate into those efforts what the partnership has come up with–what actions need to occur. Because essentially, what is needed is a top-down and bottom-up approach occurring simultaneously, and this is exactly what has been happening with the Coral Reef Initiative. However, it is a very complicated process and not easy to gain consensus among governments. Therefore, while the approaches using partnerships and consensus building are not new (for example, at the U.S. national level, partnerships were used in developing integrated coastal zone management); however, ICRI has taken these processes and principals and attempting to apply them internationally at multi-levels simultaneously.

Response: (Ismail Serageldin). There are some things that are being done, which are bound to have a profound impact, even though you don't immediately see them. One thing is what we presented at the last meeting of the CSD in April in New York, entitled *Monitoring Environmental Progress.* This is quite a revolutionary proposal which we will be discussing with the finance ministers of the world at the annual meetings [October, 1995]. This is to look not just at the greening of national income accounts, but to shift to capital accounts, and wealth accounting of nations–taking into measurement issues of natural capital, human capital, social capital–and produced assets, which is what normally is measured by economists and financial analysts. We have found very important results: that, in fact, one gets standard economic measures–such as gross domestic investment, that can look very healthy at 22 percent of Gross Domestic Product–that can actually mask a net-negative situation in terms of saving for future generations. So, if you get changes of that kind in the basic instruments that are being used to analyze macro-economic policy (which may not be immediately related to rain forests or coral reefs) it changes the whole framework in which natural resources, economic activities and investment in social activities and human beings come together. This is bound to generate a lot of change and the Bank is leading the way in many of those areas, and will continue to work with many others (that is, we are organizing a meeting with WWF) at the time of the annual CSD meeting in these issues.

Secondly, the suggestions made earlier from the ICRI process as to what the World Bank can do were quite modest and I issue a challenge to every one here: Identify countries–where you feel there is a genuine willingness on the part of the governments to work on these issues–take six, seven countries around the world that have coral reefs, that are part of the priority areas where there is an interest on the part of the government to do something, and I will be willing to talk with the Ministers of Finance. Also, we should set ourselves a target. If we can convince the Ministers of Finance in those countries to move ahead, then there is substantial funding available, depending on the level of funding of the country. Finally, in the Year of the Reef in 1997, we should aim for projects in the water and on the ground in five or six of those countries. The Bank's current project in Indonesia is, I think, a prototype of what is required, but projects do require government commitments. If governments get engaged, there really is a very large possibility of funding activities on a significant scale–to get them started, to create the framework within which these activities can move towards financial sustainability. Thus, the challenge:

- Identify countries where there is commitment and where there are priorities in terms of coral reefs.

- Communicate those that seem likely prospects. I offer to talk to the Finance Ministers during the World Bank Annual Meetings during the second week in October.

- Identify a subset where we seem to have interested governments.

- Let that subset become the target for large-scale projects to be put in place in 1996. Hopefully, by the end of 1997, we will be able to look back and say, yes, we have achieved something.

Comment: (Sophia Bettencourt). I am working in Indonesia with a coral reef project, and this is a project where the government has basically specified a cost of $120 million, of which they are willing to borrow $90 million. It is a project that they want to implement in 14 provinces starting in 33 sites. We are trying to tell them–don't go so fast, we need to get lessons of experience. My question to the team is, at this moment the government is asking for help, and I am also asking for help because we do not have lessons of experience on how to implement coral reef management. Specifically in areas where we went in the field we noticed severe problems–isolated patches of reef where there are no local communities living nearby, which are systematically being bombed, poisoned, and destroyed. How do you manage those areas? Secondly, how do you manage areas where there are no tourists–very isolated, community-based systems? Yet how do you also convince the communities to create incentives to manage the coral reefs when there is a live fish trade that serves the Hong Kong market, and where the fish is selling at excessive prices (that is, $45/kilo for live fish in Indonesia, $200/kilo in Hong Kong)? These are fish caught by cyanide poisoning. So the incentives to exploit and destroy the reefs are very, very strong. There are also very poor communities that are mining the reefs. Coral is being sold in sacks of 40 kilos for $4.00–and is much cheaper than cement. So these are the types of problems we are facing. How do we provide incentives to these communities? What alternative sources of employment can we find for them, so that we bring them into the process? NGOs and governments are not the only answer.

Response: (John McManus). I encourage you to communicate with us at ICLARM; that's what ICLARM is there for–we don't have all these answers, but we are in contact with over 6,000 people involved with coastal zone management that interact with us regularly. Secondly, as many people are not fully aware, we see the establishment of marine reserves in crowded countries as an option of coastal zone management. However, it must be part of a community development project. Today, community development relies heavily on the concept of empowerment. For example, if a local community experiences a turnover in power from an established leader, the new power base often reverts within a short time, because the newcomers have no financial base. Newcomers find themselves having to borrow money and resources from the old power base, which returns that old base to power. This cycle is very common and is a major cause of project failure. What I would suggest as a possibility for other World Bank interests might be to further explore the idea of providing loans at a very, very small scale (or support institutions, such as the Grameen Bank, which support small lending) and use this to reinforce the empowerment principle. Thirdly, if the objective of a coastal zone project is to maintain or raise the standard of living (or quality of life) of the average person, then you begin to see a line between large-scale projects which restrict access to resources of villagers, and small-scale projects which are aimed at providing livelihood and enhancing their use of those resources. For example, a five star hotel may bring in their own boatmen and employees and restrict access to the reef in front of it, with very little trickle down economic benefits. Contrast this to a series a small resorts which are organized in such a way that local fishermen are used to serve the same functions. A prime example is Apo, where the resort is clearly using locals in this way. The same dividing line tells you it is not so good to cut down mangroves to grow shrimp. Because a mangrove is always used by people whereas shrimp farming restricts access and providing very few jobs per hectare. Many of these things come down to a perception: "Who is it we're trying to help?" Is it the people who live on the coastline, or are we concentrating on a vague model of benefit from Gross National Product and foreign exchange?

Comment: (Ismail Serageldin). I am happy to report that the Board of the World Bank for the first time in the history of the Bank has approved, on March 21, a specific contribution to go directly to institutions like the Grameen Bank and we are launching the Consultative Group to Assist the Poorest (CGAP). The starting date for this is June 26, 1995, and I am chairing an NGO forum consultation on June 26, and the formal CG will be created and launched on the 27th and 28th for $100 million to reach the poorest of the poor.

Comment: (Stephen Colwell). I would like to remark on this last comment [Ismail Serageldin]; it is a wonderful development and people are looking forward to having the World Bank involved in helping to get small grant programs going. This is one of CORAL's objectives–to get small grants into places where it is difficult. The Gregor Hodgson study places an economic value in taking a fish out for a live fish trade in Hong Kong, but the value of having someone come out and see that is ten or 100 times that. However, you have to be able to present that convincingly. And you talk about areas where there is no tourism; well, one of the big developments in tourism is that's the favorite spot for people to go. So I think there is some hope. Obviously, it's not going to work in all the areas or solve all the problems, but in certain pockets it will work.

Comment: (Louise Fallon Scura). With regard to the Philippines experience, although something has innate or recognized value, to whom that value accrues is a different story. The incentives have to be in place for the people who are exploiting the resource, and they have to derive some benefit. We have a long way to go in developing such instruments. The story of small-scale fisheries is a very bleak one all the way around, and we have known this for a long time. But the problem is that there are too many fishermen chasing too few fish. Unfortunately, we are part of the problem. Before we recognized that this was a problem, we started allocating fishing rights from large-scale fishers to small-scale fishers without recognizing that at some point we couldn't use this as some sort of social sink for the unemployed. I think that we have to recognize that we have to define who the users are, and set limits for access to the resources.

With regard to the Bonaire work, we did not attempt to measure the consumer surplus there. We were actually looking to see what the perception to a potential user fee would be. Actually, we found that the dive industry had a strong misperception of what the divers actually felt about the users fee. In November, 1991 we surveyed departing tourists and learned that their attitude was not an unwillingness to pay a fee, but not if the fee was not going into direct management of a protected area. The divers were very well informed; very willing to pay to take actions that they think will have a positive impact on managing the reef, if they think the money will actually cover the cost of management.

Comment: (John Dixon). Much of the discussion has focused on a mundane, but very important issue of capturing more money from users, and particularly divers. But one shouldn't forget that a true economic analysis of the value of a coral reef is much broader than just the benefits to divers. This is only one, sometimes fairly small component, and work that has not really been reported here (and much remains to be done) offer a more complete accounting of the total range of benefits from functioning coral reef ecosystems. The Philippines have tried to do some of this in the Palauan case, and you see there are benefits to users–fishermen, divers, and local communities. Only by looking at the broader range can one decide both the incidents of benefits and costs, if those benefits are lost, as well as think of more creative ways to secure support–political, local participatory support, and money. The real challenge on the economic side is in estimating this broader range of benefits.

For divers, we can do a very good job of estimating consumer surplus–we have good techniques that are quite robust and rigorous. The numbers we are getting are fairly constant around the world. For many of the other uses–ecosystem support, habitat preservation.–it is a bit more difficult, and that's where the real challenge is on the economic side. But it is one I am hoping that we can work together with people here and in the future.

Question: I have been in the Philippines' OCES meetings and SIDS and GEF meetings in the Caribbean, and all have been on very similar topics in the last three months, and one issue that has come out clearly from all those meetings is the issue that has also come up today–it is the need to convince governments to give value to the assets which they hold. I would therefore like to ask the World Bank and the organizers of this meeting how they intend to get across to the governments of the countries which we are encouraged to identify, the value of the reef systems, so that the finance ministers may respond favorably when they meet with Mr. Serageldin in October. Is there a mechanism?

Response. (Ismail Serageldin). There is no substitute for talking face-to-face with key decisionmakers about key issues. Come October, there will be 178 finance ministers here in Washington, and I cannot meet them all. However, I would like to meet from three to ten of them during the week or so that they will be here. What I need from you is to identify those where there is a strong movement in-country (including the ministers of finance, environment, fisheries, natural resources). Where this has been identified, and there is a high priority area, I will talk to them and report back. It is a targeted approach, and not just a broadcast of intent.

Comment: (Susan Drake). For clarification on the role of governments, clearly, the ICRI has focused on governments through the Call to Action and Framework for Action; however, no matter how much government support there is, or regulations on the books, unless there is ownership by the stakeholders, you're not going to get very far [in the process].

Comment: (DeeVon Quirolo). I would like to nominate the U.S., and specifically, the world's third largest barrier reef–the Florida Keys. We have a willing government and certainly a willing local community. With regard to the diver tax discussions, I think the Florida Keys is a microcosm of this debate and Reef Relief has been party to conducting surveys, where it shows that divers have always been in favor of a diver tax, but the industry usually is not because they fear, in most cases, of being a cannibal–many of the dive operations are on a cash basis. Clearly, mechanisms can be developed to get around that, but this is where the fear comes from. But I think the whole discussion should back up one more step, and go to the varied tourist activities taking place within the coastal zone (that is, photographers, kayakers). The biggest single problem we have is coastal development, and unless we deal with the impacts and infrastructure our coral reefs will not survive. In the Keys we have a bed tax, and fortunately tourists pay for it, but unfortunately, it only goes toward advertising, and there is a great debate as to whether it should also cover services, such as sewage treatment and storm water runoff.

Comment: (Stephen Colwell). The point about broad impacts from tourism cannot be said enough. With the diving community, there seems to be some hesitation worldwide that there is this fear that [taxing, fees] will drive away business. There are economic arguments to support it, but the larger question is whether carrying capacity is being exceeded.

Comment: (Sue Wells). I would like to put in a plea to economists in the room: examples and studies on Marine Protected Areas that are protecting possibly coral reefs, but certainly other habitats that are vitally important in the conservation of coral reefs. All the studies that I am familiar with are related to coral reefs and divers and tourism. I am slightly alarmed at suggestions that tourists be sent to areas where there presently are none, and with this MPA report, we need to look at its conclusions and determine if certain areas may not be suitable for tourists, and examine how they may be made financially sustainable as well. In Belize this is a big issue, because the latest study suggests that there are certain areas that we know are very high priorities for biodiversity conservation and they are not going to be financially sustainable from tourism.

Comment: (Marea Hatziolos). I think we had a few examples of potential, in terms of mariculture, in areas that may not support tourism. Clearly, having a reef is important if you need to use the quiet backwaters; but there are other areas, for example, in West Africa where one could conceive of doing sustainable mariculture in the lagoon system.

VI. Conclusion

The Challenges Ahead

Colin Rees, Environment Department
World Bank

There will never be sufficient financial resources to address every conservation need or concern. Consequently, the challenge before us is to be creative in leveraging existing financing, converting consumer willingness to pay for exceptional natural diversity into support for its conservation, and in creating new partnerships which add value to conservation efforts through infusion of human resources and political will as well as additional financing.

We've seen today, examples of how all of these can enhance the long-term conservation of coral reef ecosystems. The Caribbean Natural Resources Institute is conducting regional seminars on sustainable revenue generation for protected areas. NGOs and the private sector are identifying investment opportunities and mobilizing venture capital for marine eco-enterprise development. The National Cancer Institute is partnering to discover new solutions in medicine, yet respecting and preserving the intellectual property of nations. The Great Barrier Reef Marine Park Authority is mentoring other nations in the establishment of marine protected areas for multiple, sustainable use.   And the International Coral Reef Initiative is actively engaging governments on a global, regional and national level to focus attention and resources on ways to reverse the decline of coral reefs worldwide.

These examples need to be built upon and replicated in the field. The successes and failures need to be documented, and the lessons learned disseminated widely to advance the next generation of ideas and actions on the ground.

Another challenge has been placed before us today. We have been asked by the World Bank's Vice President for Environmentally Sustainable Development, to identify specific opportunities for World Bank investment in countries around the world where coral reefs of exceptional importance are being threatened and where there is a strong in-country commitment to conserve these natural assets. We would therefore like to solicit proposals regarding Bank assistance for projects that would support rehabilitation, conservation and sustainable use of these ecosystems.

In pursuing these and other opportunities, our deliberations today have emphasized that to be sustainable financially and otherwise, conservation efforts must have a strong sense of ownership by those directly involved. At the local and national level, we must continue to foster a sense of participation, ownership and responsibility among stakeholders for sustainably managing those resources that directly affect the welfare and quality of life of the communities they represent. In the words of a World Bank Task Manager:

> *Through participation we lost control of the project, and in so doing, gained ownership and sustainability—precious things in our business.*

The World Bank looks forward to bringing the ideas and actions from this workshop, and the recommendations of the report, *A Global Representative System of Marine Protected Areas*, down to the local level where the decisions can be enshrined in the stewardship of natural resources by local communities. Certainly there must be other ideas and opportunities yet to identify, but this should not stop us from moving forward on the ground with the momentum generated today. We welcome your participation.

Appendix
Panel and Participant Contact Information

I. *A Global Representative System of Marine Protected Areas*

Moderator:
Jan Post
Senior Environmental Specialist, ENVLW
World Bank
1750 Pennsylvania Ave., N.W. Room S-5135
Washington, DC 20433, U.S.A.
Tel: 202-473-3400; Fax: 202 477-0568

Panelists:
Graeme Kelleher
Vice Chairman, Marine
IUCN Commission on National Parks
and Protected Areas (CNPPA)
12 Marulda St.
Aranda ACT 2614, Australia
Tel: 61-6-251-1402; Fax: 61-6-247-5761

Richard Kenchington
Senior Director
External Services Station
Great Barrier Reef Marine Park Authoriy
P.O. Box 791
Canberra, A.C.T. 2601, Australia
Tel: 61-6-247-0211; Fax: 61-6-247-5761

Chris Bleakley
Great Barrier Reef Marine Park Authority
P.O. Box 791
Canberra, A.C.T. 2601, Australia
Tel: 61-1-247-0211; Fax: 61-6-247-5761

Susan Wells
Technical Assistant
UNDP/GEF Project
Coastal Zone Management Unit
P.O. Box 1884
Belize City, Belize
Tel: 501-2-35739; Fax: 501-2-35738

II. *Financing and Sustaining Coral Reef Conservation Initiatives*

Moderator:
John Dixon, Principal Environmental
  Economist
World Bank, ENVDR
1750 Pennsylvania Ave., N.W., Room S5-045
Washington, DC 20433, U.S.A.
Tel: 202-473-8594; Fax: 202-477-0565

Panelists:
Tighe Geoghegan, Director
Institutional Development
Caribbean Natural Resources Institute
1104 Strand St., Suite 208
Christiansted, St. Croix, VI 00820
Tel: 809-773-9854; Fax: 809-773-5770

Tundi Agardy
World Wildlife Fund
R and D, Conservation Science
1250 24th St., N.W., Suite 500
Washington, DC 20037, U.S.A.
Tel: 202-861-8301; Fax: 202-293-9211

Barry Spergel
World Wildlife Fund
1250 24th St., N.W., Suite 500
Washington, DC 20037, U.S.A.
Tel: 202-293-4800; Fax: 202-861-8324

Kathy Mikitin, Operations Specialist
World Bank, ENVGC
1750 Pennsylvania Ave., N.W., Room S2-139
Washington, DC 20433, U.S.A.
Tel: 202-473-2910; Fax: 202-522-3256

Kathy MacKinnon, Biodiversity Specialist
World Bank, ENVGC
1750 Pennsylvania Ave., N.W., Room S2-129
Washington, DC 20433, U.S.A.
Tel: 202-458-4682; Fax: 202-552-3256

III. *Income Generating Opportunities and Environmental Limitations*

Moderator:
Louise Fallon Scura, Natural Resource
  Management Specialist
World Bank, ENVLW
1750 Pennsylvania Ave., N.W., Room S5-109
Washington, DC 20433, U.S.A.
Tel: 202-458-1921; Fax: 202-477-0568

Panelists:
David Newman
Division of Cancer Treatment
National Cancer Institute
Cancer Research and Development Center
P.O. Box B
Frederick, MD 21702-1201, U.S.A.
Tel: 301-846-5387; Fax: 301-846-6178
Email: Newman@dtpvx2.ncifcrf.gov

Walter Adey
Museum of Natural History
Smithsonian Institution
Washington, DC 20516, U.S.A.
Tel: 202-357-1860; Fax: 202-357-3037

John Walch, President
SeaPhix, L.L.C.
8102 West Columbine
Peoria, AZ 85345, U.S.A.
Tel: 602-412-1301; Fax: 602-412-1491
Email: Wavemanaz@aol.com

Billy Causey, Superintendent
Florida Keys National Marine Sanctuary
NOAA-National Ocean Services
Sanctuaries and Reserves Division
P.O. Box 500368
Marathon, FL 33050, U.S.A.
Tel: 305-743-2437; Fax: 305-743-2357

Ricardo Meléndez-Ortiz, Director General
Fundación Futuro Latinamericano
Av. Amazonas 3741 y Corea
Office 52, Piso 5
Quito, Ecuador
Tel: (593 2) 435 521; Fax: (593 2) 462 204

IV. *Creating a Planning and Investment Framework through Partnerships*

Moderator:
John McManus, Reefbase Project Leader
International Center for Living Aquatic
  Resources Management
MC P.O. Box 2631
Makati, Metro Manila 0718, Philippines
Tel: 63-2-818-0466; Fax: 63-2-816-3183

Panelists:
Michael Rubino
International Finance Corporation
1850 I Street, N.W.
Washington, DC 20433, U.S.A.
Tel: 202-473-2891; Fax: 202-334-8705

Michael Pearson, Project Manager
Ras Mohammed National Park
Sector Development Project
Sharm el Sheikh P.O. Box 19
South Sanai, Egypt
Tel: 20-62-600559; Fax: 20-62-600668

Robert Kerr, Manager
Protected Areas Resource Conservation
  Project
Planning Institute of Jamaica
8 Ocean Blvd.
Kingston, Jamaica
Tel: 809-967-3689; Fax: 809-967-4915

Hank Cauley
Biodiversity Conservation Network
Biodiversity Support Program
c/o World Wildlife Fund
1250 24th St., N.W., Suite 500
Washington, DC 20037, U.S.A.
Tel: 202-293-4800; Fax: 202-861-8324

V. *Group Discussion*

Moderator:
Marea Hatziolos, Coastal and Marine
  Resources Management Specialist
World Bank, ENVLW
1750 Pennsylvania Ave., N.W., Room S5-141
Washington, DC 20433, U.S.A.
Tel: 202-478-5779; Fax: 202-477-0568

Panelists:
Susan Drake, Coordinator
International and U.S. Coral Reef Initiative
ICRI, U.S. Department of State
OES/ETC, Room 4325
2201 C St., N.W.
Washington, D.C. 20520, U.S.A.
Tel: 202-647-3078; Fax: 202-647-5247

Stephen Colwell, Executive Director
The Coral Reef Alliance
809 Delaware St.
Berkeley, CA 94710, U.S.A.
Tel: 510-528-2492; Fax: 510-528-9317
Email: CoralReefA@aol.com

VI. *Workshop Participants*

Constance Arvis, Science Officer
U.S. Department of State
2201 C St., N.W., Room 5805
Washington, D.C. 20520, U.S.A.
Tel: 202-647-9532; Fax: 202-647-1106

David Attaway
NOAA
1305 East-West Highway
Silver Spring, MD 20910, U.S.A.
Tel: 301-713-2451, ext. 154

Miriam Baltuck, Chief
Oeans, Mission to the Planet Earth
NASA Headquarters, Code YSC
Washington, DC 20546, U.S.A.
Tel: 2002-482-6196; Fax: 202-482-4307

Sofia Bettencourt
World Bank, EA3AG
700 18th St., N.W., Room MC9-446
Washington, DC 20433, U.S.A.
Tel: 202-478-2554

Barry Blake
Overseas Development Administration
Barbados
Fax: 809-426-2194

Karla Boreri
University of Rhode Island - Coastal
  Resources Center
Graduate School of Oceanography
Coastal Resources Center
Narragansett, RI 02882, U.S.A.
Tel: 401-792-6224 Fax: 401- 789-4670

Robin Broadfield, Regional Coordinator
World Bank, ENVGC
1750 Pennsylvania Ave., N.W., Room S2-131
Washington, DC 20433, U.S.A.
Tel: 202-473-4355; Fax: 202-522-3256

Stephen Cairns
Smithsonian Institution, W-329
Department of Invertebrate Zoology
NHB-163
Washington, DC 20516, U.S.A.
Tel: 202-786-2129; Fax: 202-357-3043

Phillip Church
USAID, CDIE
Room 220, SA-18
Washington, DC 20523-1802, U.S.A.
Tel: 703-875-4972; Fax: 703-875-4866

David Clark, Assistant to the Executive
 Director
Office of the Executive Director
World Bank
701 19th Street, N.W.
Room E-1123
Washington, DC 20433, U.S.A.
Tel: 202-458-1071; Fax: 202-477-2007

Shannon Clearly, Chief
Office of International Affairs–023
National Park Service, Int'l Affairs
P.O. Box 37127
Washington, DC 20013-7127, U.S.A.

Gary Costello, Consultant
World Bank
1919 Pennsylvania Ave., N.W., Room Q7-
 167
Washington, DC 20433, U.S.A.
Tel: 202-473-1913; Fax: 202-522-3132

Michael Crosby, Co-Chair
Domestic Management for Sustainable Use
 Task Group, NOAA, OCRM
Ocean and Coastal Resource Management
NOAA, SSMC-4, Room 11536
Silver Spring, MD 20910, U.S.A.
Tel: 301-713-3155, ext. 114; Fax: 713-4012
Email: mcrosby@coasts.nos.noaa.gov

Clif Curtis
Greenpeace International
1436 U Street, N.W.
Washington, DC 20009, U.S.A.
Tel: 202-462-1177; Fax: 202-462-4507

Carlos de Paco
AVINA c/o The Nature Conservancy
1815 North Lynn St.
Arlington, VA 22209, U.S.A.
Tel: 703-841-4599; Fax: 703-841-4880

Mark Dillenbeck
National Environmental Fund Initiative,
 IUCN
1400 16th St., Suite 502
Washington, DC 20036-2266, U.S.A.
Tel: 202-797-5454; Fax: 202-797-5461

Paula DiPerna
The Cousteau Society
777 United Nations Plaza
New York, NY 10017, U.S.A.
Tel: 212-949-6290; Fax: 212-949-6296

Mark Eakin, Co-Chair
Research Assessment and Monitoring Task
 Group, Office of Global Programs, NOAA
1000 Wayne Ave., Suite 1225
Silver Spring, MD 20910-5603, U.S.A.
Tel: 301-427-2089; Fax: 301-427-2073
Email: eakin@ogp.noaa.gov

N.B. Fanning, Co-Chair
Domestic Management for Sustainable Use
 Task Group
U.S. Dept. of Interior
Territorial and International Affairs
1849 C St., MS 4328
Washington, DC 20240, U.S.A.
Tel: 202-208-6816; Fax: 202-501-7759

Candy Feller
Smithsonian Institution
Environmental Research Center
P.O. Box 28
Edgewater, MD 21037, U.S.A.
Fax: 301-261-7954

Fritz Fischer, Executive Director for
 Germany
World Bank
701-19th Street, N.W., Room E1-325
Washington, DC 20433, U.S.A.
Tel: 202-478-1183; Fax: 202-477-7849

John Fritts
American Fisheries Society
5410 Grosvernor Lane, #10
Bethesda, MD 20814, U.S.A.
Tel: 301-897-8616; Fax: 301-987-8096

Yves Gillet
CREOCEAN
Allee des Tamaris
17000 La Rochelle
France
Tel: 33-46-41-1313; Fax: 33-46-505-102

Gina Green, Director
Jamaica and Belize Country Programs and
 Protected Areas
The Nature Conservancy
1815 North Lynn St.
Arlington, VA 22209, U.S.A.
Tel: 703-841-5366; Fax: 703-841-4880

Lynne Hale, Associate Director
Coastal Resources Center
Graduate School of Oceanography
University of Rhode Island
Narragansett, RI 02882, U.S.A.
Tel: 401-792-6224; Fax: 401-789-4670

Lee Hannah
Conservation International
1015 18th St., N.W., Suite 1000
Washington, DC 20036, U.S.A.
Tel: 202-429-5660; Fax: 202-887-5188

Phillip Hazelton
World Bank, LA3AG
1850 I St., N.W., Room I5-059
Washington, DC 20433, U.S.A.
Tel: 202-473-4804; Fax: 202-522-3540

Maureen Hearn
Defenders of Wildlife
1244 19th St., N.W.
Washington, DC 20036, U.S.A.
Tel: 202-659-9510; Fax: 202-833-3349

Richard Hellman, President
United States Committee for the United
 Nations Environment Programme
2013 Q St., N.W.
Washington, DC 20009, U.S.A.
Tel: 202-234-3600; Fax: 202-332-3221

Frank Hicks
Biodiversity Conservation Network
c/o World Wildlife Fund
1250 24th St., N.W., Suite 500
Washington, DC 20037, U.S.A.
Tel: 202-293-4800; Fax: 202-861-8324

Porter Hoagland
Woods Hole Oceanographic Institute
Marine Policy Center
Woods Hole, MA 02543, U.S.A.
Tel: 508-457-2867; Fax: 508-457-2184

Brenda Holland
NOAA, Ocean and Atmospheric Research
NOAA/OGP-1305 East-West Highway
Silver Spring, MD 20910, U.S.A.
Tel: 301-713-1193

Anthony Hooten, Consultant
AJH, Environmental Services
4005 Glenridge Street
Kensington, MD 20895-3708, U.S.A.
Tel: 301-942-8839; Fax: 301-942-8839
Email: 76260.2413@compuserve.com

Sarwat Hussain, External Affairs Officer
World Bank, ESDVP
1818 H St., N.W.
Washington, DC 20433, U.S.A.
Tel: 202-473-5690; Fax: 202-473-3112

Stephen Jameson, Coastal Resources
Management Advisor
NOAA, OCRM
1305 East-West Highway
Silver Spring, MD 20910, U.S.A.
Tel: 301-713-3086, ext. 206; Fax: 301-713-
4370

James Johnson, International Affairs
Specialist
NOAA, International Affairs
14th and Constitution Ave.
NOAA–DAS, Room-5230
Washington, DC 20230, U.S.A.
Tel: 202-482-6196; Fax: 202-482-4307

Nels Johnson
World Resources Institute
1709 New York Ave., Suite 700
Washington, DC 20006, U.S.A.
Tel: 202-662-2529; Fax: 202-638-0036

Sally Johnson
CTEED, International Finance Corporation
1850 I St., N.W., Room I10-149
Washington, DC 20433, U.S.A.
Tel: 202-473-3390; Fax: 202-676-9495

John Kermond
NOAA/OGP
1100 Wayne Ave., Suite 1225
Silver Spring, MD 20910, U.S.A.
Tel: 301-427-2089, ext. 22; Fax: 301-427-2082

Kevin Kirby, Principal
Land Ethics, Inc.
424 4th St., Suite C
Annapolis, MD 21703, U.S.A.
Tel: 410-267-6272; Fax: 410-267-6248

Rosemary Krussman, Conservation
  Coordinator
National Aquarium in Baltimore
Pier 3-501 East Pratt St.
Baltimore, MD 21202, U.S.A.
Tel: 410-659-4207; Fax: 410-576-8238

Stephen Lintner, Principal Environmental
  Specialist
World Bank, ENVLW
1750 Pennsylvania Ave., N.W., Room S5-121
Washington, DC 20433, U.S.A.
Tel: 202-473-2508; Fax: 202-477-0568

Shoshanna Mallett, Counsel
United States Committee for the United
  Nations Environment Programme
2013 Q St., N.W.
Washington, DC 20009, U.S.A.
Tel: 202-234-3600; Fax: 202-332-3221

Will Martin, Deputy Assistant Director
NOAA, International Affairs
14th and Constitution Ave.
Room-5230, HCHB
Washington, DC 20230, U.S.A.
Tel: 2002-482-6196; Fax: 202-482-4307

Joan Martin-Brown,
Advisor to the Vice President
World Bank, ESVDP
1750 Pennsylvania Ave, N.W., Room S7-039
Washington, DC 20433, U.S.A.
Tel: 202-473-2310; Fax: 202-473-3112

Betsy McGean
World Bank, EC4HM
Room H-5200
600 19th Street, N.W.
Washington, D.C. 20433, U.S.A.
Tel: 202-458-5576, Fax: 202-522-1165

Phil McGillivary
Management Technology
1313 Locust Ave.
Fairmont, WV 26554, U.S.A.
Tel: 304-367-1699; Fax: 304-367-1759

Dean Milliken, Associate Director
Florida Institute of Oceanography
University of South Florida
830 First St., S
St. Petersburg, FL 33701, U.S.A.
Tel: 813-893-9100; Fax: 813-893-9109

Robert Milne, Special Advisor
National Park Service, Intl. Affairs
Office of International Affairs–023
P.O. Box 37127
Washington, DC 20013-7127, U.S.A.

Ken Newcomb, Chief
World Bank, ENVGC
1750 Pennsylvania Ave., N.W., Room S2-141
Washington, DC 20433, U.S.A.
Tel: 202-473-6010; Fax: 202-522-3256

Brad Northrup, Vice President and Director
  of Caribbean Region
The Nature Conservancy
1815 North Lynn St.
Arlington, VA 22209, U.S.A.
Tel: 703-841-5366; Fax: 703-841-4880

Stephen Parcells
National Audubon Society
801 Pennsylvania Ave., SE, Suite 200
Washington, DC 20003, U.S.A.
Tel: 202-547-9009; Fax: 202-547-9022

Arthur Paterson
NOAA, International Affairs
14th and Constitution Ave., N.W.
Room-5230, HCHB
Washington, DC 20230, U.S.A.
Tel: 202-482-6196; Fax: 202-482-4307

Richard Paton
International Waters
World Bank, ENVGE
1750 Pennsylvania Ave., N.W., Room S2-147
Washington, DC 20433, U.S.A.
Tel: 202-473-3585; Fax: 202-522-3256

Bill Patzert
NOAA, Satellite Oceanography
NOAA/OGP-1305 East-West Highway
Building 4, Rm 8402
Silver Spring, MD 20910, U.S.A.
Tel: 301-713-1193

Esther Peters
Tetra Tech, Inc.
10360 Eaton Place, Suite 340
Fairfax, VA 22030, U.S.A.
Tel: 703-385-6000; Fax: 703-385-6007

Kennard Potts
U.S. Environmental Protection Agency
401 M Street, SW, 4504 F
Washington, DC 20460, U.S.A.
Tel: 202-260-7893; Fax: 202-260-9960

Allen Putney
International Union for the Conservation of
  Nature
1400 16th St., Suite 502
Washington, DC 20036-2266, U.S.A.
Tel: 202-797-5454; Fax: 202-797-5461

Carlos Quintela
AVINA c/o The Nature Conservancy
1815 North Lynn St.
Arlington, VA 22209, U.S.A.
Tel: 703-841-4599; Fax: 703-841-4880

Deevon Quirolo, Project Director
Reef Relief
P.O. Box 340
Key West, FL 33041, U.S.A.
Tel: 305-294-3100; Fax: 305-293-9515

Gil Radonski
Sport Fishing Institute
1010 Massachusetts Ave., N.W., Suite 100
Washington, DC 20001, U.S.A.
Tel: 703-519-9691; Fax: 703-519-1872

Colin Rees, Chief
World Bank, ENVLW
1750 Pennsylvania Ave., N.W., Room S5-143
Washington, DC 20433, U.S.A.
Tel: 202-458-2715; Fax: 202-477-0568

Walter Reid
World Resources Institute
1709 New York Ave., N.W., Suite 700
Washington, DC 20006, U.S.A.
Tel: 202-638-6300; Fax: 202-638-0036

Klaus Reutzler
W-330, Smithsonian Institution
Department of Invertebrate Zoology, NHB-
  163
Washington, DC 20516, U.S.A.
Tel: 202-786-2129; Fax: 202-357-3043

Chonlada Sae-Hau
World Bank, ESVDP
1750 Pennsylvania Ave., N.W., Room S7-040
Washington, DC 20433, U.S.A.
Tel: 202-478-1971; Fax: 202-473-3112

Richard Schwabacher
The Cousteau Society
777 United Nations Plaza
New York, NY 10017, U.S.A.
Tel: 212-949-6290; Fax: 212-949-6296

Janice Sessing
NOAA, Sanctuaries and Reserves
Technical Projects Branch
1305 East-West Highway, 12th floor
Silver Spring, MD 20910, U.S.A.

Ismail Serageldin, Vice President
World Bank, ENVSD
1818 H St., N.W.
Washington, DC 20433, U.S.A.
Tel: 202-473-5690; Fax: 202-473-3112

Ann Shulman, Assistant Director
The Coral Reef Alliance
809 Delaware St.
Berkeley, CA 94710, U.S.A.
Tel: 510-528-2492; Fax: 510-528-9317

Lars Soeftestad, Anthropologist
World Bank, ENVSP
1750 Pennsylvania Ave., N.W., Room S5-040
Washington, DC 20433, U.S.A.
Tel: 202-473-8263; Fax: 202-522-3247

Fred Sowers
Tufts University
Department of Environmental Studies
Tel: 202-362-3341

Andrew Steer, Director
World Bank, ENV
1818 H St., N.W., Room S5-055
Washington, DC 20433, U.S.A.
Tel: 202-473-3299; Fax: 202-477-0565

Achim Steiner
International Union for the Conservation of
  Nature
1400 16th St., N.W., Suite 502
Washington, DC 20036-2266, U.S.A.
Tel: 202-797-5454; Fax: 202-797-5461

Phillip Taylor
National Science Foundation
4201 Wilson Blvd., Room 725
Arlington, VA 22230, U.S.A.
Tel: 703-306-1587; Fax: 703-306-0390
Email: prtaylor@nsf.gov

John Tschirky
The Nature Conservancy
1815 North Lynn St.
Arlington, VA 22209, U.S.A.
Tel: 703-841-5366; Fax: 703-841-4880

Erik van de Linde
Embassy of the Netherlands
4200 Linnean Ave., N.W.
Washington, DC 20008, U.S.A.
Tel: 202-244-5300; Fax: 202-966-0728
Email: P00807@PSLINK.COM

Rien Van Wier
Embassy of the Netherlands
4200 Linnean Ave., N.W.
Washington, DC 20008, U.S.A.
Tel: 202-244-5300; Fax: 202-966-0737

Susan Ware
NOAA, International Affairs
14th and Constitution Ave
Room-5230, HCHB
Washington, DC 20230, U.S.A.
Tel: 2002-482-6196; Fax: 202-482-4307

John Waugh
International Union for the Conservation of
  Nature
1400 16th St., N.W., Suite 502
Washington, DC 20036-2266, U.S.A.
Tel: 202-797-5454; Fax: 202-797-5461

Peter Weber
Worldwatch Institute
1776 Massachusetts Ave., N.W.
Washington, DC 20036, U.S.A.
Tel: 202-452-1999; Fax: 202-296-7635

Anthony Whitten
ASTEN
World Bank
700 18th St., N.W., Room MC8-439
Washington, DC 20433, U.S.A.
Tel: 202-458-2253

Distributors of World Bank Publications

ARGENTINA
Carlos Hirsch, SRL
Galeria Guemes
Florida 165, 4th Floor-Ofc. 453/465
1333 Buenos Aires

Oficina del Libro Internacional
Alberti 40
1082 Buenos Aires

AUSTRALIA, PAPUA NEW GUINEA, FIJI, SOLOMON ISLANDS, VANUATU, AND WESTERN SAMOA
D.A. Information Services
648 Whitehorse Road
Mitcham 3132
Victoria

AUSTRIA
Gerold and Co.
Graben 31
A-1011 Wien

BANGLADESH
Micro Industries Development
    Assistance Society (MIDAS)
House 5, Road 16
Dhanmondi R/Area
Dhaka 1209

BELGIUM
Jean De Lannoy
Av. du Roi 202
1060 Brussels

BRAZIL
Publicacoes Tecnicas Internacionais
    Ltda.
Rua Peixoto Gomide, 209
01409 Sao Paulo, SP

CANADA
Le Diffuseur
151A Boul. de Mortagne
Boucherville, Québec
J4B 5E6

Renouf Publishing Co.
1294 Algoma Road
Ottawa, Ontario K1B 3W8

CHINA
China Financial & Economic
    Publishing House
8, Da Fo Si Dong Jie
Beijing

COLOMBIA
Infoenlace Ltda.
Apartado Aereo 34270
Bogota D.E.

COSTA RICA, BELIZE, GUATE -MALA, HONDURAS, NICARAGUA, PANAMA
Chispas Bookstore
75 Meters al Norte del Hotel Balmoral
    en calle 7
San Jose

COTE D'IVOIRE
Centre d'Edition et de Diffusion
    Africaines (CEDA)
04 B.P. 541
Abidjan 04 Plateau

CYPRUS
Center of Applied Research
Cyprus College
6, Diogenes Street, Engomi
P.O. Box 2006
Nicosia

CZECH REPUBLIC
National Information Center
P.O. Box 668
CS-113 57 Prague 1

DENMARK
SamfundsLitteratur
Rosenoerns Allé 11
DK-1970 Frederiksberg C

EGYPT, ARAB REPUBLIC OF
Al Ahram
Al Galaa Street
Cairo

The Middle East Observer
41, Sherif Street
Cairo

FINLAND
Akateeminen Kirjakauppa
P.O. Box 23
FIN-00371 Helsinki

FRANCE
World Bank Publications
66, avenue d'Iéna
75116 Paris

GERMANY
UNO-Verlag
Poppelsdorfer Allee 55
53115 Bonn

GREECE
Papasotiriou S.A.
35, Stournara Str.
106 82 Athens

HONG KONG, MACAO
Asia 2000 Ltd.
46–48 Wyndham Street
Winning Centre
7th Floor
Central, Hong Kong

HUNGARY
Foundation for Market Economy
Dombovari Ut 17-19
H-1117 Budapest

INDIA
Allied Publishers Private Ltd.
751 Mount Road
Madras - 600 002

INDONESIA
Pt. Indira Limited
Jalan Borobudur 20
P.O. Box 181
Jakarta 10320

IRAN
Kowkab Publishers
P.O. Box 19575-511
Tehran

IRELAND
Government Supplies Agency
4-5 Harcourt Road
Dublin 2

ISRAEL
Yozmot Literature Ltd.
P.O. Box 56055
Tel Aviv 61560

R.O.Y. International
P.O. Box 13056
Tel Aviv 61130

Palestinian Authority/Middle East
Index Information Services
P.O.B. 19502 Jerusalem

ITALY
Licosa Commissionaria Sansoni SPA
Via Duca Di Calabria, 1/1
Casella Postale 552
50125 Firenze

JAMAICA
Ian Randle Publishers Ltd.
206 Old Hope Road
Kingston 6

JAPAN
Eastern Book Service
Hongo 3-Chome, Bunkyo-ku 113
Tokyo

KENYA
Africa Book Service (E.A.) Ltd.
Quaran House, Mfangano St.
P.O. Box 45245
Nairobi

KOREA, REPUBLIC OF
Daejon Trading Co. Ltd.
P.O. Box 34
Yeoeida
Seoul

MALAYSIA
University of Malaya Cooperative
    Bookshop, Limited
P.O. Box 1127, Jalan Pantai Baru
59700 Kuala Lumpur

MEXICO
INFOTEC
Apartado Postal 22-860
14060 Tlalpan, Mexico D.F.

NETHERLANDS
De Lindeboom/InOr-Publikaties
P.O. Box 202
7480 AE Haaksbergen

NEW ZEALAND
EBSCO NZ Ltd.
Private Mail Bag 99914
New Market
Auckland

NIGERIA
University Press Limited
Three Crowns Building Jericho
Private Mail Bag 5095
Ibadan

NORWAY
Narvesen Information Center
Book Department
P.O. Box 6125 Etterstad
N-0602 Oslo 6

PAKISTAN
Mirza Book Agency
65, Shahrah-e-Quaid-e-Azam
P.O. Box No. 729
Lahore 54000

Oxford University Press
5 Bangalore Town
Sharae Faisal
P.O. Box 13033
Karachi-75350

PERU
Editorial Desarrollo SA
Apartado 3824
Lima 1

PHILIPPINES
International Book Center
Suite 720, Cityland 10
Condominium Tower 2
Ayala Avenue, H.V. dela
    Costa Extension
Makati, Metro Manila

POLAND
International Publishing Service
Ul. Piekna 31/37
00-577 Warszawa

PORTUGAL
Livraria Portugal
Rua Do Carmo 70-74
1200 Lisbon

SAUDI ARABIA, QATAR
Jarir Book Store
P.O. Box 3196
Riyadh 11471

SINGAPORE, TAIWAN
Gower Asia Pacific Pte Ltd.
Golden Wheel Building
41, Kallang Pudding, #04-03
Singapore 1334

SLOVAK REPUBLIC
Slovart G.T.G. Ltd.
Krupinska 4
P.O. Box 152
852 99 Bratislava 5

SOUTH AFRICA, BOTSWANA
Oxford University Press
    Southern Africa
P.O. Box 1141
Cape Town 8000

SPAIN
Mundi-Prensa Libros, S.A.
Castello 37
28001 Madrid

Libreria Internacional AEDOS
Consell de Cent, 391
08009 Barcelona

SRI LANKA & THE MALDIVES
Lake House Bookshop
P.O. Box 244
100, Sir Chittampalam A.
    Gardiner Mawatha
Colombo 2

SWEDEN
Fritzes Customer Service
Regeringsgatan 12
S-106 47 Stockholm

Wennergren-Williams AB
P.O. Box 1305
S-171 25 Solna

SWITZERLAND
Librairie Payot
Case postale 3212
CH 1002 Lausanne

Van Diermen Editions Techniques
P.O. Box 465
CH 1211 Geneva 19

TANZANIA
Oxford University Press
Maktaba Street
P.O. Box 5299
Dar es-Salaam

THAILAND
Central Books Distribution Co. Ltd.
306 Silom Road
Bangkok

TRINIDAD & TOBAGO, JAMAICA
Systematics Studies Unit
#9 Watts Street
Curepe
Trinidad, West Indies

UGANDA
Gustro Ltd.
1st Floor, Room 4, Geogiadis Chambers
P.O. Box 9997
Plot (69) Kampala Road
Kampala

UNITED KINGDOM
Microinfo Ltd.
P.O. Box 3
Alton, Hampshire GU34 2PG
England

ZAMBIA
University Bookshop
Great East Road Campus
P.O. Box 32379
Lusaka

ZIMBABWE
Longman Zimbabwe (Pte.) Ltd.
Tourle Road, Ardbennie
P.O. Box ST 125